RELIGION ON TRIAL

RELIGION ON TRIAL

How Supreme Court Trends Threaten the Freedom of Conscience in America

Phillip E. Hammond
David W. Machacek
Eric Michael Mazur

ALTAMIRA
PRESS

A Division of Rowman & Littlefield Publishers, Inc.
Walnut Creek • Lanham • New York • Toronto • Oxford

ALTAMIRA PRESS
A division of Rowman & Littlefield Publishers, Inc.
1630 North Main Street, #367
Walnut Creek, California 94596
www.altamirapress.com

Rowman & Littlefield Publishers, Inc.
A wholly owned subsidiary of
The Rowman & Littlefield Publishing Group, Inc.
4501 Forbes Boulevard, Suite 200
Lanham, Maryland 20706

PO Box 317
Oxford
OX2 9RU, UK

British Library Cataloguing in Publication Information Available

Library of Congress Cataloging-in-Publication Data

Hammond, Phillip E.
    Religion on trial : how Supreme Court trends threaten freedom of
conscience in America / Phillip E. Hammond, David W. Machacek, Eric
Michael Mazur.
        p. cm.
Includes bibliographical references (p.   ) and index.
    ISBN 0-7591-0600-2 (cloth) — ISBN 0-7591-0601-0 (pbk.)
    1. Freedom of religion—United States. 2. United States. Supreme
Court. I. Machacek, David W. II. Mazur, Eric Michael. III. Title.

    KF4783 .H36 2004
    342.7308'52—dc22

                                                            2003021821

Printed in the United States of America

∞™ The paper used in this publication meets the minimum requirements of
American National Standard for Information Sciences—Permanence of Paper
for Printed Library Materials, ANSI/NISO Z39.48-1992.

[T]he American Creed facilitates the appeal from the actual to the ideal. When we talk of the American democratic faith, we must understand it in its true dimensions. It is not an impervious, final and complacent orthodoxy, intolerant of deviation and dissent, fulfilled in flag salutes, oaths of allegiance, and hands over the heart. It is an ever-evolving philosophy, fulfilling its ideals through debate, self-criticism, protest, disrespect, and irreverence; a tradition in which all have rights of heterodoxy and opportunities for self-assertion. The Creed has been the means by which Americans have haltingly but persistently narrowed the gap between performance and principle.

—Arthur M. Schlesinger Jr.
The Disuniting of America

Contents

Foreword

Religious freedom is one of America's most cherished traditions. Religious historian Sanford Cobb once referred to the American tradition of religious freedom as "America's greatest contribution to human civilization." Cobb was surely right in his assessment, as it has been the United States which has led the way in enshrining religious freedom as a basic human right, sacred in itself, which must be protected from powerful but sometimes misdirected governmental authorities. Yet the task is not as easy as it sounds. Good people disagree over the meaning of religious freedom, how best to protect religious freedom, how far persons should be given the freedom to practice unorthodox religions, whether religious pluralism is compatible with religious freedom, the degree to which government should play a role in acknowledging or promoting religion, and even whether nations themselves are religious or secular entities. Each generation of Americans is responsible for both preserving and contributing to our tradition of religious freedom. Because protecting religious freedom is difficult, there is always the danger that religious freedom is in peril. I agree with the authors that we are presently experiencing such a time when our first freedom—religious freedom—is seriously in peril. This book explains why, and tells Americans what they must do to protect their great tradition of religious freedom.

This book possesses the rare virtue of having been written for the general public. Legal professionals and scholars have been debating church-state issues for all of American history, but the insights of those debates have seldom reached the public. It is important that the public understand these debates because their votes, especially in national elections, have a powerful influence on those who make and shape law and thus on the direction of religious freedom in the United States. It is not in the halls of academia that important decisions about the direction of U.S. law are made, but in the realm of public discourse. Here, Hammond, Machacek, and Mazur address the public with their concerns about the future direction of church-state jurisprudence. I would encourage every American to read this book before he or she votes. It may have a strong influence on the persons we put into public office.

The authors believe deeply in a much maligned doctrine, the separation of church and state. They believe that the greatest liberty is afforded by leaving matters of conscience for the individual to decide, and removing government's ability to interfere with those decisions. On this point, they "take alarm at the presence in our government—indeed, on the Supreme Court, an institution charged with protecting our liberty from arbitrary laws—of some who would erode that liberty by allowing voting majorities to impose their own moral judgments—often derived from sectarian religious beliefs— on others, who would erode that liberty by allowing greater government regulation and endorsement of religion, indeed who deny the very principles from which religious liberty was derived."

Indeed, what Justice Sandra Day O'Connor has referred to as "well-settled First Amendment jurisprudence, Supreme Court decisions that once upheld church-state separation as the inviolable method of protecting religious freedom," is now being eroded, slowly and almost imperceptibly, but nevertheless eroded. This process of erosion, of decline, needs to be understood, widely understood, lest we lose our way and one day discover that religious freedom is a thing of the past. This book will do much to reawaken Americans, reawaken them to protecting the one principle—religious freedom—that has been most responsible for making America one of the great political experiments in human history.

Derek H. Davis
Director, J. M. Dawson Institute of Church-State Studies
Baylor University
Waco, Texas

Preface

Collaboration is not at all uncommon for academic writers, but this particular collaboration is unusually meaningful because it grew out of an unusually strong relationship between a mentor and two of his students. The book was conceived at a party celebrating Phillip Hammond's retirement from a remarkably productive forty-two-year academic career. During that event, for which several of Hammond's former students had returned to Santa Barbara, California, the question was raised whether he planned to continue writing after retirement. No one was surprised to learn that he would continue writing—for many of us, writing is not so much a job as a habit—and the conversation turned to possible topics. During that conversation, the suggestion was made that some of what he had already said to academic audiences ought to be said to the general public also. We had in mind his writings on church-state issues and, in particular, two recent essays on shifts in church-state jurisprudence at the Supreme Court. These form the basis of chapters 5, 6, and 7 of this book.

In retrospect, we might have expected that Hammond's reply would consist of an invitation to collaborate. Having previously collaborated with him on other projects and having developed our understanding of church-state issues under Hammond's tutelage, David Machacek and Eric Michael Mazur eagerly accepted. In a sense, therefore, this book represents a passing of responsibility for a tradition of knowledge from one generation to the next, a responsibility not merely to preserve that tradition but also to build upon it.

In many ways, the story of how this book was conceived is analogous to the story we tell in the book. We contend that the Bill of Rights was never intended to put the matter of rights to rest but rather to ensure that the debate over rights would continue beyond the founding generation; thus, that Americans' understanding of their rights would continue to evolve. Indeed, the Founders thought, wisely, that the rights of the people of the United States would be *better* protected by a lively and ongoing public discourse about rights than by words on paper. The example of the declarations of rights in the state constitutions had demonstrated the futility of what James Madison called "parchment barriers" to the abuse of rights. To whatever extent a national bill of rights was going to be successful, it would be by generating among Americans a spirit of reverential respect for rights rather than by setting down in precise wording what those rights were or placing specific legal restrictions on the powers of government. The *spirit* of the Constitution and Bill of Rights was, in the minds of the Framers of American government, more powerful than the letter of the law. Although we discuss the intentions of the Framers, therefore, we do not share the mistaken belief, so common in political rhetoric today, that knowing the intentions of the Founders absolves us of thinking for ourselves about these issues.

Each generation of Americans inherits a tradition of rights and the responsibility for both preserving and contributing to that tradition. As in academic disciplines, this passing of the mantle of freedom involves both promise and peril. There is promise in that the present generation may discover new meanings of liberty or that they may correct prior misunderstandings. But there is also the risk that, in passing custodianship of rights from one generation to the next, something of great importance will be lost. We fear that the freedom of conscience is now in jeopardy, and we hope that this book helps to turn this perilous tide.

Introduction

In August 2003, Roy Moore, the chief justice of the Alabama State Supreme Court, defied a federal court ruling and the consensus of his judicial peers by refusing to remove a nearly three-ton monument of the Ten Commandments that he had installed in the rotunda of the Alabama Supreme Court building. Earlier that summer, the U.S. Supreme Court declared unconstitutional a Texas law prohibiting same-sex sodomy, a decision that liberal-minded Americans praised as ending government sponsorship of a sectarian moral code and conservatives condemned as hostility toward "traditional" religious values. A year earlier, in July 2002, the decision of a federal circuit court declared unconstitutional the practice of reciting the Pledge of Allegiance in public schools because it contains the words "under God." These events, unsurprisingly, set off controversy nationwide, as advocates for a greater role for religion in public life battled advocates of greater church-state separation.

Tellingly, people on both sides in these debates articulated their positions in terms of First Amendment protections of religious liberty. Other issues were involved, of course—issues such as the intervention of the federal government in the states and the power of courts to overrule the will of the majority. But to the minds of most Americans, the core issue was the freedom of religion, and people on both sides of these, and similar, debates saw themselves as defending the freedom of religion. There is only a very radical minority in the United States who advocate *less* religious freedom—those who would dismantle the First Amendment and establish their own religion as the official religion of the nation. This book is not written for them. It is written, rather, for the overwhelming majority of Americans who believe in religious freedom but may disagree about how best to protect and preserve it.

Indeed, there are probably finer points on which we, the authors, may not fully agree. However, we have come to a consensus on the central theme of this book, which is that what the First Amendment protects is the freedom of conscience. And the purpose of this book is to explain how we arrived at this conclusion, what it means for contemporary debates about church-state issues, and why we believe it leads to the greatest liberty and justice for all, which, we assume, is the end desired by virtually all Americans.

Although scholarship led us to the argument presented in this book, we write here not as scholars but as citizens and as advocates of the separation of church and state. The considerations presented herein have led us to believe that the greatest liberty is afforded by leaving matters of conscience for the individual to decide. And we take alarm at the presence in our government—indeed, on the Supreme Court, an institution charged with protecting our liberty from arbitrary laws—of some who would erode that liberty by allowing voting majorities to impose their own moral judgments, often derived from sectarian religious beliefs, on others, who would erode that liberty by allowing greater government regulation and endorsement of religion, indeed, who deny the very principles from which religious liberty was derived.

We suffer no illusions about the fact that some, having considered our position and having recognized some of its implications, will continue to disagree with us. We can only hope that their dissent will be based on a conscientious and reasoned assessment of what approach to church-state relations will best further the ideals of liberty rather than on intentional ignorance and bigotry.

This book is organized around a premise that we believe is central to American history and culture—the premise that, from the beginning of this nation, changes in society have been mainly in the direction of greater and greater individual freedom. These changes have, of course, often been resisted, but freedoms, once won, have not been revoked except under extraordinary circumstances, such as during war when, for example, restrictions were placed on travel and rationing was imposed.

Our premise is nicely illustrated by the remarks of President George W. Bush following Senator Trent Lott's egregiously segregationist statements in December 2002 at Senator Strom Thurmond's birthday party. Bush said, "Recent comments by Senator Lott do not reflect the spirit of our country. . . . Every day our nation was segregated was a day that America was unfaithful to our founding ideals."[1] No one, we submit, would take Bush to be saying that segregation and segregationists no longer exist; rather, he is identifying a promise of freedom inherent in the founding of the United States, a promise that has been sought, partially met, and is still being pursued. Put another way, George Bush is implying that these "founding ideals" really exist, even if they are not always practiced.

There is, however, another implication in Bush's remarks that Bush himself probably does not understand—that changes made in the direction of our founding ideals cannot be reversed without violating those ideals. Thus, when Bush calls for the return of prayers to the public schools, for the deregulation of rapacious corporations, or for restrictions on women's reproductive rights, he is misunderstanding American history and culture in the same way Trent Lott does. There *is* direction to changes in American society that accord with the ideals identified in the Declaration of Independence and given organizational form in the U.S. Constitution.

We are not so naïve as to think these changes cannot be neutralized, even reversed. When that happens, however, notice will be taken and appeals to the "founding ideals" will be invoked. As Justice Sandra Day O'Connor said in her concurring opinion to Justice Antonin Scalia's majority opinion in the 1990 *Smith* decision (that ignored many prior free exercise precedents pertinent to that case), it "dramatically departs from well-settled First

Amendment jurisprudence . . . [and] is incompatible with our Nation's fundamental commitment to individual religious liberty." But that opinion was written by Justice Scalia who, as we shall see later, shows many signs of not believing in any *natural* right to religious liberty.

Nor are we "triumphalist" in imagining that America's founding ideals will fully prevail. We are guided rather by the notion that a choice made at one time will inexorably set in motion the forces that create choices to be made at a later time. The fulcrum choice at the center of our book is the 1940 *Cantwell* decision that unanimously declared the right of a Jehovah's Witness to solicit without a city license because he was *religiously* motivated. This decision overturned—in the direction of greater religious liberty—a precedent that had been followed since 1879. But this choice eventually forced onto the Supreme Court's agenda two additional issues that could not be dodged. One issue was the question of limitations. Obviously, religious motivation cannot justify just any action, but on what basis can it be limited? The second issue forced onto the Court by *Cantwell* was the question of *when* such motivation could be regarded as truly religious. Reluctant in the past to define what *is* religious, the justices came to regard conviction or conscience as the functional equivalent of religion and a characteristic that *could* be defined without entangling the Court in questions of religious truth.

Our argument is organized in three parts. First, we examine the origin of the U.S. Constitution and Bill of Rights. Since the regressive turn in current Supreme Court jurisprudence is usually carried out in the name of the Framers' "original intent," we look for what must have been the thinking of the Framers of the Constitution as they set up a tripartite government of checks and balances. We look especially at the role of the judicial branch and conclude that the Framers would applaud the expanded notion of religious liberty that emerged in twentieth-century jurisprudence.

Second, we look at the record of the judicial system from 1789 through the 1930s. We learn that the narrow understanding of the First Amendment advocated by today's regressive justices does not reflect the thinking or intentions of the eighteenth-century Framers of the Constitution and Bill of Rights but rather reflects an understanding of church and state that emerged in the nineteenth century.

Third, we look closely at the last half century of U.S. Supreme Court decisions on church-state issues, seeing them as a critical battleground for progressives who would further expand religious liberty and for regressives who would subject that liberty to majority rule.

The resolution of these two issues in favor of an ever-expanding religious freedom—what Justice O'Connor calls "well-settled First Amendment jurisprudence"—is now under assault. Religious liberty or conscience is in jeopardy, threatened by those who in our view woefully misconstrue the course of religious freedom in America.

Notes

1. *New York Times*, 13 December 2002, 1, 22.

1

Powers, Rights, and Freedoms

Americans have always been quick to claim, but slow to understand, their rights. Even in colonial times, colonial governors complained that Americans were always clamoring about their rights (Hutson 1991). However, when it came to expressing what those rights were, even articulate spokesmen for the cause of rights, such as James Madison who introduced the Bill of Rights to Congress in 1789, found it difficult to do. Among the more common complaints about the declarations of rights contained in the various state constitutions was that they were incomprehensible to most citizens. How could Americans protect and preserve their rights if they did not know what those rights were? By what means could a claim of rights be evaluated? How could legitimate claims of rights be sorted out from illegitimate ones; a genuine right from a mere selfish interest?

These kinds of difficulties, in fact, underlay resistance by many in the early Republic to adding a bill of rights to the federal Constitution. Some, Madison himself, thought that a bill of rights was both unnecessary and potentially dangerous. They thought that the Constitution conferred only very limited powers on the federal government. Indeed Federalists thought that the Constitution so severely constrained the powers of the federal government that it would prove ultimately ineffective—potentially too weak to protect the rights of the people, much less to pose a danger to them. Others took the demand for a bill of rights as evidence that the democratic spirit had not yet fully sunk into the American mind. A letter to the *Pennsylvania Gazette* on January 9, 1788, for example, declared: "Let these truths sink deep into our hearts: that the people are masters of their rulers . . . and that a master reserves to himself . . . everything else which he has not committed to the care of those servants" (quoted in Rutland 1955: 151). Furthermore, an enumeration of rights could easily be misconstrued as an exclusive list, as had happened in many of the state constitutions, so that those rights that were not listed were understood to have been given up. A list of rights could, in other words, be taken as the *only* rights enjoyed by the people, implying power where power was not given. Writing in *The Federalist* in 1780, for instance, Alexander Hamilton worried that bills of rights were

> not only unnecessary in the proposed Constitution, but would even be dangerous. They would contain various exceptions to powers not granted; and, on this very account, would afford a colorable pretext to claim more than were granted. For why declare that things shall not be done which there is no power to do? Why, for instance, should it be said that the liberty of the press shall not be restrained, when no power is given by which restrictions may be imposed? (Quoted in Rutland 1955: 182)

Perhaps the most influential argument against a bill of rights was given by James Wilson in a speech in Philadelphia during the ratification process:

> it would have been superfluous and absurd, to have stipulated . . . that we should enjoy those privileges, of which we are not divested. . . . But in a government of enumerated powers, such as is proposed for the United States, a bill of rights would not only be unnecessary, but, in my humble judgment, highly imprudent. . . . A bill of rights annexed to the constitution is an enumeration of the powers reserved. If we attempt an enumeration, everything that is not enumerated is presumed to be given. The consequence is, that an imperfect enumeration would throw all implied power into the scale of the government, and the rights of the people would be rendered incomplete. On the other hand, an imperfect enumeration of the powers of government reserves all implied power to the people; and by that means the constitution becomes incomplete.

> But of the two, it is much safer to run the risk on the side of the constitution; for an omission in the enumeration of the powers of government is neither so dangerous nor important as an omission in the enumeration of the rights of the people. (Quoted in Rogge 1960: 13)

Madison fully accepted this argument until political necessity and the influence of his mentor Thomas Jefferson convinced him that, if the Federalist argument that a government of enumerated powers lacked the ability to harm rights was true, then a bill of rights could do no harm and might have, in Madison's words, "a salutary effect against the abuse of power" by the executive and legislative branches of government (quoted in Rogge 1960: 17).

When Madison undertook to compose a bill of rights, therefore, he faced a daunting task. Either he had to compose an extensive, and, one would hope, complete list of rights to be preserved, or he had to compose a bill of rights that would protect rights that he might overlook or, more likely, rights he could not foresee. A bill of rights that was not constructed with the greatest of care could be potentially dangerous to the rights of the people. A narrowly conceived bill of rights would provide little protection, especially when the government was acting in the name of the voting majority.[1]

Knowing this, and knowing of the considerable debate that went into the final wording of the Bill of Rights before it was amended to the Constitution in 1791, gives us reasonable cause to think that selective use of certain words was significant to the authors and worthy of closer examination by those of us today who wish to understand better the authors' intent. This chapter describes the selective use of three words in the Constitution and Bill of Rights: "power," "right," and "freedom."

The "Power" of the Federal Government

One of the most striking features of the Constitution of 1789, especially given Americans' concerns at the time about protecting their rights against a powerful federal government, is the near total absence of any reference to rights in the original Constitution.

Indeed, the word "right" appears only once. Article I, section 8, empowers the Congress to "promote the Progress of Science and useful Arts by securing for limited Times to Authors and Inventors the exclusive Right to their respective Writings and Discoveries." By contrast, the word "power" appears sixteen times. "Freedom" makes no appearance at all, although the Preamble assures that one of the purposes of the federal government is to "secure the Blessings of Liberty."

Are we to take this to mean that the Founders were unconcerned about the impact that a federal government would have on the rights of the American people? It seems almost silly to ask that question given the reasons stated in the Declaration of Independence for the American Revolution (that governments are instituted for the purpose of securing "certain unalienable rights"), the constant clamoring over rights in the public, and the fact that John Locke's *Two Treatises on Government* for a time informed as many sermons in American pulpits as the Bible.[2] However, it was not a silly question then, when anti-Federalists accused Federalist advocates of the Constitution of attempting to thwart the principles of the Revolution as stated in the Declaration of Independence—which had by then been accepted as the ideal toward which American government should strive—by creating a potentially tyrannical federal government. And it is not a silly question now, when debates rage over the proper extent and limit of federal power and the proper interpretation of the Constitution of the United States in courts of law.

Understanding what the composers of the 1789 Constitution intended requires some grounding in eighteenth-century political philosophy. The notable influences then are still familiar today: Hobbes, Locke, and Rousseau. These philosophers posited that the origins of government could be found when humans emerged out of a "state of nature" and entered into a "social contract." In a state of nature, humans enjoy perfect freedom to act on self-interest, desire, and impulse. In other words, if I am hungry, and I see someone else with an apple, I am free to try to take it from him. In a state of nature, no law prevents my theft (or rape, or murder) except, potentially, the laws of nature—if he is stronger than I am, I will probably walk away hungry and possibly injured. This is clearly an undesirable state because, although I am perfectly free to do whatever I will, including to steal, murder, and rape, everyone else is also free to murder, rape, or steal from me.

A much more desirable state of affairs can easily be achieved if the parties involved agree not to steal from each other, to murder one another, or to rape each other. This "social contract" is the origin of government. In a social contract, humans voluntarily give up some of their freedom in order to be free from certain evils.

There are several peculiar features of this understanding of the origins and purpose of government. First, on a shallow level, it means that government and social order are human creations, as opposed to being divinely ordained. This has serious implications, since it also means that government and social order are a product of negotiation, and that therefore they are subject to renegotiation and change. This philosophy of government explodes the notion of an ontologically fixed, ideal system of government (whose origins lay in divine command or some other source). This marks a significant departure from the philosophy of government that dominated in medieval Europe. The notion of a "good society," therefore, becomes religiously and morally neutral. Rather than one that conforms to the dictates of divine command as revealed in the Bible or in the traditions of the church, the good society is simply the system in which the greatest number of individuals can gain the greatest benefit with the least cost to their personal freedom—the system to which the greatest number of freely acting individuals, acting on their own self-interest, can voluntarily consent.

This points to a second peculiar feature, more profound, which is the consensual nature of government. In order to be truly consensual, the freely acting individual must be free to enter the contract, but also to evacuate it under certain circumstances. One such circumstance is articulated in the Declaration of Independence—when a powerful group usurps freedoms that other participants in the contract have not voluntarily given up. Humans give up certain freedoms when they enter a social contract *in order to protect others*, and when the government fails to protect those freedoms, or, worse, becomes corrupted by rulers who would deliberately remove them, then participants are justified in evacuating the contract, that is, to engage in revolution.

But there is a third peculiar feature of this thinking of the Framers of the Constitution that helps us understand that word "unalienable," now generally written as "inalienable." Not all rights were created by consensus, nor were they consequences of a "social contract." The Framers were not followers of Rousseau, imagining society as *only* a social contract. Instead they envisioned a society designed to protect rights in the *nature* of what it means to be human—"natural" rights. The Federalist writers of the 1789 Constitution, having this understanding of the conception of government in mind—indeed, having been committed to such an understanding by their complicity in the American Revolution—found no need to dwell on the matter of rights and freedoms in the Constitution because they understood that the federal government would be limited to those powers expressly given over to it by the people in the Constitution. These powers were very specific and limited in scope. So limited were they, in fact, that Federalists feared they had created an ineffectual government and called therefore for strengthening that government by conferring more powers on it than already bestowed. Most important, they understood that those freedoms not given up to the federal government as "powers" conferred on it by the Constitution were retained by the people or, if conferred by the people on their respective state governments, retained by the states.

Given this understanding, the notion that the Constitution needed a bill of rights was seen by many thoughtful advocates of democracy as utterly preposterous. The rights of the people consisted of everything that they had *not* conferred on the federal government. And, as already mentioned, a bill of rights could create the impression that those rights enumerated as being reserved to the people were their *only* rights; that, in other words, those rights not reserved had been given up. This was the exact opposite of what the Constitution's writers had intended by creating a government of enumerated powers.

This background helps us to understand better the sometimes puzzling language of the Bill of Rights itself. It has been noted by other scholars that the Bill of Rights was written as an argument against the declarations of rights imbedded in the constitutions of the states (Hutson 1991). By declaring certain positive rights, these constitutions gave the impression both of exclusiveness and of having been conferred by the state on its citizens, an indulgence of the state. That understanding of rights was directly contrary to the understanding of rights expressed in the Declaration of Independence. The danger to rights did not derive from the form of government—monarchy, aristocracy, dictatorship, or popular democracy. The danger came from misunderstanding the origin of rights: if it was understood that rights were conferred by the state, then they could also be legitimately and justly abridged or taken away by the state.

Indeed, this reasoning stood behind the rejection of the Massachusetts state constitution by the citizens of Ipswich. They objected to the fact that, as worded, the state constitution's Declaration of Rights "allowed" the right of a free religious conscience, "when, in fact, the free exercise and enjoyment is the natural and uncontrollable right of every member of the state" (quoted in Rutland 1955: 67). These citizens were not objecting to religious freedom; they objected to the implication that religious freedom could be granted by the state, when in fact that freedom is natural and inalienable. The Declaration of Independence declared that certain rights are prior to the state and cannot be taken away by the state. It asserted, furthermore, that when a state attempts to remove such rights, the people are justified in taking up arms against it. In objecting to the wording of the Massachusetts constitution, these citizens were echoing the ideals articulated in the Declaration of Independence, which had already become established in the still-emerging national culture. The debate over the wording of the Massachusetts constitution concerned not whether citizens of that state should enjoy the right of a free conscience but rather where that right should be located in a hierarchy of value.

The assertion that some rights are inalienable goes two ways. Some rights, implicitly, are *alienable*—that is, they can be given up by consent of the governed and they can, under some circumstances, such as criminal or treasonous behavior, be taken away by the state. Other rights are *inalienable*—they can neither be given up, nor, under any circumstances, be taken away by the state. These inalienable rights are properly conceived, not as "civil" rights, but as "natural" or "human" rights. The former, civil rights, are those that citizens enjoy by virtue of their participation in a particular kind of social contract, and they concern, foremost, the rights of the individual in his or her relationship to the state (for instance, the right to vote or the right to trial by jury). A citizen of one state might, therefore, be entitled to certain civil rights that he or she might not enjoy under a different political system. Natural or human rights are of a higher order in that they are understood to be the right of all humans regardless of their participation in any particular kind of social contract. These rights are inherent in all humans and, indeed, are part of what it means to be human. They are therefore both universal and inalienable. Like the right of a free conscience, people cannot possibly give up such rights and these rights cannot possibly be taken away—one can disallow behavior expressive of a belief, but one cannot control belief itself.

This distinction—no small one—was in circulation at the time the Bill of Rights was composed. For instance, delegates to the Delaware convention took an oath to act on behalf of the "natural, civil, and religious rights and privileges" of citizens when composing that state's constitution. And the town of Beverly rejected the proposed constitution of the state of Massachusetts on the grounds that it failed to "describe the Natural Rights of Man as he inherits them from the Great Parents of Nature, distinguishing those, the control of which he may part with to society from those he cannot" (quoted in Rutland 1955: 55, 56). The distinction, furthermore, is made in the Bill of Rights, and it becomes evident when we examine the selective use of the term "right" in these amendments to the U.S. Constitution.

The Bill of "Rights"

Surprisingly, the word "right" appears only six times in the Bill of Rights. The First Amendment refers to the "right of the people peaceably to assemble, and to petition the Government for a redress of grievances." The Second Amendment protects "the right of the people to keep and bear Arms." "The right of the people to be secure in their persons, houses, papers, and effects, against unreasonable searches and seizures" is guaranteed by the Fourth Amendment. The Sixth Amendment affirms the right of those accused of a crime to a speedy, public trial by an impartial jury, to be informed of the nature and cause of the accusation, to be confronted with witnesses against him, to obtain witnesses for his defense, and to have assistance of legal counsel. The Seventh Amendment guarantees the right to a trial by jury in civil cases. And finally, the Ninth Amendment refers to "certain rights" that are not listed in the Constitution.

The right to vote, of course, does not appear in the Constitution until after the Civil War in 1868. Even then, the reference in the Fourteenth Amendment concerns the suspension of voting rights of convicted felons. The right to vote then makes several appearances. The Fifteenth Amendment (1870) extends the right to vote to people of color; the Nineteenth Amendment (1920) extends voting rights to women; the Twenty-fourth Amendment (1964) outlaws poll taxes; and the Twenty-sixth Amendment (1971) lowers the age of eligibility to vote to eighteen.

The case of voting rights is telling, for it suggests the alienability of those rights that receive the name of "rights" in the Constitution. The right to vote was not seen by the Founders, or by later Americans, as inherent to all humans. They could foresee circumstances in which the right to vote might be withheld or withdrawn. Even today, we speak of "eligibility" to vote, suggesting that some persons are appropriately ineligible to vote (because of age or because of their criminal activities).

Each of the instances in which a "right" is enumerated in the Bill of Rights concerns, in some fashion, the relationship of the individual to the government. They are rights that are enjoyed by virtue of one's citizenship in good standing in the United States of America. Obviously, these rights cannot be thought to exist in a "state of nature." One cannot, for instance, vote in a state of nature because there is no government; one cannot expect a fair trial by an impartial jury because there are no courts. In a sense, these rights are created by the social contract; one *gains* them by entering into the social contract.

Furthermore, each of the "rights" listed in the Bill of Rights concerns matters on which reasonable persons can agree that there are circumstances that would justify their removal or withdrawal. Even the most hardened advocate of the Second Amendment would agree, one hopes, that violent criminals should not be allowed to keep and bear arms. The voting rights of people convicted of felony crimes are suspended. And at times of war or imminent danger to the nation, habeas corpus rights may be suspended (although this is always controversial).

The most important quality of the "rights" listed in the Bill of Rights is that they are subject to change as a result of renegotiation. A citizen might enjoy rights in this country that are not enjoyed by citizens in another; or she may enjoy rights now that her ancestors did not. (He may also enjoy rights now that his descendents will not. We are reminded that the price of liberty is vigilance.)

Remaining, of course, are those rights that are held most dear by Americans—religious and associational freedom, freedom of the press, and so on. Are these not also civil rights? Why does the Bill of Rights not name them as such? Indeed, they are not *civil* rights because, unlike the rights discussed above, which one gains upon entry into the social contract, these rights are understood by the Bill of the Rights to exist *prior to government*. The Bill of Rights refers to them, not as "rights," therefore, but as "freedoms," or more generally as "liberty."[3] These are rights of a higher order, therefore, than civil rights. They are not thought to derive from one's citizenship in a particular system of government, but are rather understood to derive from the fact of one's humanity. They are therefore universal, inalienable, and non-negotiable.

The distinction being made here between civil rights and "freedoms," or rights of a higher order, is evident in the First Amendment:

> Congress shall make no law respecting an establishment of religion, or prohibiting the free exercise thereof; or abridging the freedom of speech, or of the press; or the right of the people peaceably to assembly, and to petition the Government for a redress of grievances.

Here, the "freedom" of religion, speech, and press is distinguished from the "right" of peaceful assembly and to petition for redress of grievances.

The language of rights used in the Constitution, therefore, suggests a hierarchy of value. The "powers" vested in the federal government in the 1789 Constitution consist of those rights that are relinquished by the people to the government and, indeed, rights that it is probably in the best interests of the people to relinquish for the sake of "domestic Tranquility," "the common defense," and the "general Welfare"—the power to wage war, regulate interstate commerce, and set standards of measure, for instance. The "rights" preserved by the people in the Bill of Rights are those that arise as a result of entering into a particular kind of social contract. These are, in a real sense, not only protections from the power of government, but also the powers to be enjoyed by the people in their government—the right to vote, to petition for redress of grievances, and so on. These rights, like the powers of the federal government, are subject to renegotiation and change as provided for in Article V of the Constitution. Indeed, this is how the power of amendment has typically been used in American history—to reform the process of election (Amendment XII) and to expand voting rights, as already discussed. But the Constitution and Bill of Rights distinguishes these lower-order rights from "freedoms" or rights of the highest order, which are thought to be inherent in human nature, inalienable therefore, non-negotiable, and thus beyond the reach of legislation.

It may be noted that the above leaves several matters specified for protection in the Bill of Rights unaccounted for. Missing are the protection from being forced to house soldiers (Amendment III); the protections from being held without indictment, from "double jeopardy," from self-incrimination, from deprivation of life, liberty, or property without due process, and from conscription of private property without compensation (Amendment V); and the protections from excessive fines and cruel and unusual punishment (Amendment VIII). These matters receive neither the name of "freedom" nor of "rights." Where, then, do they stand in the hierarchy of value?

On the one hand, the rights in question concern, primarily, the individual's relationship to the state and have, therefore, an intuitive connection with the civil "rights" protected in other amendments. That is, they are protections from arbitrary use of the power of government. The difference is that, unlike the "rights" protected in other amendments, the positive right that is being protected is not articulated. These amendments deviate from the pattern in other amendments in which a positive right is asserted and then protected by restrictions on the power of government. For example, the Fourth Amendment asserts the positive "right of the people to be secure in their persons, houses, papers, and effects" and protects that right by prohibiting the state from search and seizure without a legal warrant. Amendments III, V, and VIII prohibit certain actions by the state without first asserting what the positive right being protected is. As such, we might conclude that these unnamed rights are *civil* rights, or rights of a lower order.

On the other hand, however, the inclusion of the holy trinity—life, liberty, and property—in the Fifth Amendment suggests that the rights in question are considered more fundamental, rights of a higher order. The "right" to due process is therefore a means of protecting "liberty"—a lower-order right is brought into the service of higher-order rights.

Perhaps the best answer that can be given using the hierarchy of value as an interpretive lens is that the status of these rights is not made clear by the language used to describe them in the Bill of Rights. Like other amendments, the language leaves these matters open to a certain amount of interpretation, a feature that largely accounts for the resilience of the Bill of Rights through changing historical circumstances over the course of American history. The vagueness of the Bill of Rights—what, for instance, constitutes a "liberty"?—has meant that Americans have not had to pass new constitutional amendments every time a question of rights arose. It can certainly be said that whatever the status of these rights in the minds of the authors of the Bill of Rights, they have *come to be seen* as sacred highest-order rights by subsequent generations of Americans, being typically included—with the exception of forced housing of soldiers—with highest-order rights in Americans' understanding of fundamental human rights as standards against which the justice of governments can be judged.

Let us turn our attention, finally, to the Ninth and Tenth Amendments. The meaning of these two amendments has often eluded citizens and scholars alike. They read as follows:

> Amendment IX: The enumeration in the Constitution, of certain Rights, shall not be construed to deny or disparage others retained by the people.
> Amendment X: The powers not delegated to the United States by the Constitution, nor prohibited by it to the States, are reserved to the States respectively, or to the people.

The complementary nature of these amendments is intuitively clear, and the distinction between "rights" and "powers" made in the forgoing pages is reiterated, but what do these amendments actually mean?

Two insights into these amendments follow from the discussion above. First, they reiterate the argument of the Federalists at the time that only those rights designated as powers of the federal government have been given up upon ratification. All powers not conferred on the federal government by the Constitution are retained as rights by the people or, as designated in the constitutions of the various states, by the states. In other words, the federal government has *only* those powers designated to it by the Constitution. New powers may be added, but only by consent of the people as set out in Article V. Remember, however, that only some of these retained rights can be turned over by consent of the governed; others are inalienable. The federal government is thus portrayed, not as an autonomous entity, but as entirely dependent for its powers on the consent of the people; it is utterly prevented from employing other powers, even if citizens would wish to grant those powers to government. The spirit of the Revolution, in other words, persists in these amendments.

This insight illuminates the meaning of the Ninth Amendment, which offers a blanket answer to the question, "What are the rights of the people?" That answer is simply "certain inalienable rights (freedoms)" plus "everything that they have not conceded" to their federal or state government, whether explicitly listed for protection in the Constitution or not (Hutson 1991). Amendment IX resolves a problem that must have given Madison many sleepless nights, that is, that an enumeration of rights designated for protection under the Constitution would inevitably leave out something (such as the right of privacy, which does not appear in the Constitution but which was, nonetheless, inferred by the Supreme Court in *Griswold v. Connecticut*, 1965, a case involving a law that forbid the use of contraception; the right to privacy also served as the basis of the Court's decision in *Roe v. Wade*, 1973). The Ninth Amendment absolved Madison of the task of attempting to compile a complete list of all the rights—natural and civil—of the people, of ranking them on the hierarchy of value described above, and of convincing Congress and then three-fourths of the states to amend each to the Constitution. One can imagine that, absent the Ninth Amendment, the task of developing and promoting a bill of rights would have consumed the remainder of Madison's life, and probably the lives of many congressional officeholders for generations to come. The Ninth Amendment not only allows, it *assumes* that people have rights in addition to those specifically mentioned in the Constitution.

This raises a second point about the meaning of the Ninth and Tenth Amendments. These Amendments are an invitation to continue the conversation about rights that gave rise not only to the Bill of Rights itself but also to the American Revolution and the republican system of government designed for the newly liberated states. The subject of rights was then, and continues to be now, a difficult one to master, and few if any would have claimed a sufficient mastery of the subject of rights to have the final, authoritative say; Madison included. What limited understanding of rights anyone in the early Republic had, what limited understanding they had of how to form a "more perfect Union, establish Justice, . . . and secure the Blessings of Liberty" was a product of the lively public debate over rights that characterized the era; one that took place, notably, in the institutions of religion, voluntary political and fraternal associations, and the press, as well as through review of claims of right by the judiciary. Indeed, this may partially explain the privileged position in the Bill of Rights of prohibitions against government interference in the realm of public discourse. The Bill of Rights, in brief, begins—in the First Amendment—by singling out for protection a realm in which matters of conscience, rights, and freedom could be publicly discussed and debated; it ends—in the Ninth and Tenth Amendments—by asserting that the debate is not over just because the Constitution now had a Bill of Rights.

Third, this leads to the inevitable conclusion that disputes over "inalienable freedoms" were not in the jurisdiction of legislatures, let alone popular opinion, but were to be adjudicated in constitutional, "natural law" terms. That is, the Constitution reflects the idea, stated explicitly in the Declaration of Independence, that the law (i.e., human legislation) is accountable to a higher law (that is natural or human rights). Or, in other words, the Framers were concerned about setting up some mechanism for evaluating the justice of laws, and that role was assigned to the Supreme Court. Why the current Chief Justice of the U.S. Supreme Court repudiates this principle is discussed elsewhere in this volume.

However, a fourth point must be made about how the meaning and intent of the Bill of Rights foreshadows the Chief Justice's position. Having only recently cast off the yoke of an oppressive national government, eighteenth-century Americans were suspicious of the idea of a powerful national government. They saw state governments as the protectors of their rights against encroachment by the federal government. The attempt by Federalists to strengthen the federal government by supplanting the Articles of Confederation with a new federal Constitution stimulated fear, therefore, about the possible erosion of rights under the new system, and this fear led to the popular demand for a bill of rights, which was seen—foremost—as restricting the powers of the newly established constitutional government. In addition to assuring Americans—in the first eight amendments—that the federal government would not intrude on those rights that Americans held most dear, the Bill of Rights addressed their fears by reaffirming—in the Ninth and Tenth Amendments—the sovereignty of the states in all matters not specifically designated to the federal government by the Constitution.

Conclusion

Eighteenth-century political philosophy held that the origins of government lay in the emergence of humans from a state of nature into a social contract. By entering into a social contract, humans give up some of their freedoms in exchange for the protection of others. The Constitution is clearly such a contract, and the rhetorical use of the words "power," "right," and "freedom" sheds light on the meaning of that contract. It says, in essence, that the people of the United States give up certain lesser freedoms in order to protect freedoms that they hold to be of higher, indeed ultimate, value.

This has several implications, but none so important as this: By setting up a hierarchy of rights, in which certain rights— natural, human, or inalienable rights—are held to be ultimate and prior to government, the Constitution, as amended in 1791 to include the Bill of Rights, provides a basis for evaluating the justice of the law, the justice of the government, indeed the justice of the Constitution itself.

Indeed, one suspects that Madison may have intended the Bill of Rights as something of an argument for the justice of the Constitution. Madison himself thought a bill of rights was unnecessary and potentially dangerous. He undertook the task in order to placate anti-Federalist critics of the Constitution who accused him and other Federalist advocates of the Constitution of tyrannical motives. But, in the end, Madison had the final say, which has come down to us in the form of the Ninth and Tenth Amendments, which, as pointed out by James Hutson on the 200th anniversary of the ratification of the Bill of Rights, consist of a "repetition of the argument used by the Federalists to repudiate a bill of rights" (1991: 69). That argument is, in effect, that the powers of the government are entirely dependent on the consent of the people, but the rights of the people are entirely immune to the powers of the government.

The period lasting from just prior to the American Revolution until ratification of the Bill of Rights represents the first major moment in the history of Americans' understanding of rights. Prior to 1776, when Americans claimed their rights were being violated by the colonial governments, they were claiming their rights *as English citizens* and as guaranteed by the colonial charters, Magna Charta, and English common law (Rutland 1955: 26–27). By 1776, as reflected in the Declaration of Independence, Americans were claiming their "unalienable" rights as human beings, written in the "laws of Nature and of Nature's God," as well. By 1789, it was clear that Americans understood certain rights to be sacred, and they demanded guarantees that the newly created constitutional government would respect them. The result was the Bill of Rights, which reflected the hierarchy of value that had evolved in the Americans' understanding of rights during this period.

As argued above, the First Amendment stands out, not merely in the order of its appearance in the Bill of Rights[4] but, more important, in the hierarchy of value. The freedoms described there—freedom of religion, freedom of speech, and freedom of the press—are elevated to a special status in the Bill of Rights; these fundamental, human rights are prior to government, inherent and inalienable, beyond dispute, and thus beyond the reach of legislation. Indeed, they represent, in the words of George Mason who authored the Virginia Declaration of Rights on which the Bill of Rights was largely modeled, "enchanted ground" (quoted in Rutland 1955: 40).

As we will see, the regressive bloc on the current Supreme Court has largely abandoned this understanding of rights. Specifically, espousing a philosophy of "legal realism," they deny the distinction between inalienable "freedoms," or in more contemporary parlance "liberty rights," and "civil rights." From their perspective, we have only civil rights, or rights created by our particular system of government. If the majority of the voting population wishes to grant certain rights, they may employ the democratic process to *create* such rights. However, to these justices, rights are limited to those specifically enumerated in the Constitution; there are no natural freedoms that exist prior to and transcend the written law. When the Court has acknowledged these unwritten "liberty rights," the regressive justices have accused their colleagues of "judicial activism," of creating new rights without going through the proper legislative channels. It should be obvious that this position repudiates the very foundation of the Constitution and Bill of Rights. We return to these matters in chapters 5, 6, and 7.

Notes

1. Indeed, we see in later chapters that the regressive bloc on the Supreme Court today advocates such a narrow interpretation of the Bill of Rights.

2. We may exaggerate, but see Barbara McGraw, *Rediscovering America's Sacred Ground* (2003).

3. In Supreme Court jurisprudence, one frequently finds references to certain "liberty rights," a term that is not precisely equivalent to "freedom" or "liberty" as used in the Constitution but carries much the same meaning in that it usually refers to rights that are not specifically mentioned in the Constitution, but are understood as fundamental rights immune to the power of legislation. As we see in later chapters, regressive justices on the current Supreme Court deny the existence of "liberty rights."

4. The First Amendment was actually the third of twelve amendments originally sent to the states for ratification. The first two amendments dealt with matters of apportionment and salary increases for Congress (see chapter 3).

2

Religious Liberty and the Freedom of Conscience

In the previous chapter we argued that the First Amendment protections enjoy a privileged status in the Bill of Rights. But what exactly does the First Amendment protect? The thesis of this book is (1) that the First Amendment protects the freedom of conscience—broadly understood as the "moral powers of rationality and reasonableness in terms of which persons define personal and ethical meaning in living"(Richards 1999: 86)—and (2) that therefore Supreme Court decisions that further restrict government sponsorship of religion and decisions that expand the free exercise of religion are consistent with the meaning and intent of the First Amendment. Correlatively, those decisions that allow government sponsorship and restrict free exercise run counter to the tradition of expanding religious liberty set in motion by the First Amendment.

Our argument rests on the interpretation of a mere forty-five words—the words of the First Amendment, whose authors saw fit to leave deliberately brief, vague, and therefore open to multiple interpretations. Indeed, the chapters that follow show how much the Supreme Court's interpretation of the First Amendment has changed over the course of American history. Typically the pattern of changing interpretations has been in the direction of greater expansion of liberty and lesser state sponsorship of religion, at least until recently. We are arguing, further, that, while the earlier pattern represents the gradual unfolding of the First Amendment's intent, the recent regressive trend in church-state jurisprudence violates the principles of the First Amendment. If the First Amendment is vague and open to interpretation, however, on what basis are we justified in this argument?

Fortunately, the Framers of the U.S. Constitution left a considerable body of commentary on the subject of religious liberty and the freedom of conscience. In this chapter, we examine some of this commentary in order to understand better the philosophical underpinnings of the First Amendment.[1] We look especially at those documents that exerted the greatest influence on the development of the First Amendment and ultimately secured its passage as a statement of one of the most fundamental principles of American government: that religion "must be left to the conviction and conscience of every man; and it is the right of every man to exercise it as these may dictate. . . . [T]hat in matters of Religion, no man's right is abridged by the institution of Civil Society and that Religion is wholly exempt from its cognizance"(James Madison, "To the Honorable General Assembly of the Commonwealth of Virginia a Memorial and Remonstrance," reprinted in Alley 1985: 56; hereafter "Memorial and Remonstrance").[2] Specifically, we argue that the principle of religious freedom grew out of the recognition that conscience is inherently immune from coercion. The freedom of conscience, in other words, was one of those inalienable rights spoken of in the previous chapter, which people cannot possibly relinquish to civil government. As an expression of conscience, it stood to reason that religion should be immune to the coercive powers of government. As we will see, James Madison and Thomas Jefferson—the two most important influences on the First Amendment—explicitly opposed interpretations of religious freedom that are now in ascendance in the Supreme Court.

James Madison on Religious Liberty

James Madison was by far the most influential advocate of religious liberty in the early Republic, and also the most articulate exponent of the principles that guided the drafting of the First Amendment. Early in his career as a statesman, Madison's correspondence with friends revealed his concerns about attempts by the Episcopal Church—then the established church of Virginia, Madison's home state—to dominate the religious discourse and to persecute conscientious dissenters.

In correspondence with William Bradford, a friend from college, Madison decried the far-reaching effects that a religious establishment could have. In his mind, the problem was not only the injustice of religious persecution and intolerance, which he certainly abhorred, but also the effects that such an establishment had on industriousness, virtue, commerce, and the arts. Bradford was fortunate, Madison wrote, to live in Pennsylvania:

> You are happy in dwelling in a Land where those inestimable privileges are fully enjoyed and [the] public has long felt the good effects of their religious as well as Civil Liberty. Foreigners have been encouraged to settle among you. Industry and Virtue have been promoted by mutual emulation and mutual Inspection, Commerce and the Arts have flourished, and I can not help attributing those continual exertions of Genius which appear among you to the inspiration of Liberty and that love of Fame and Knowledge which always accompany it. Religious bondage shackles and debilitates the mind and unfits it for every noble enterprise, every expanded prospect. (Reprinted in Alley 1985: 50)[3]

Clearly, to Madison, religious intolerance was an intrinsic evil to be combated, but it was also only one manifestation of an even deeper evil, which contemporary scholars have described as moral or intellectual "slavery" (Richards 1999). In short, religious persecution was evil, in Madison's thinking, because it violated the freedom of conscience.

From Conscience to the Free Exercise of Religion

To understand better Madison's thinking on the subject, we have only to look a little further back in his biography, to his education at Princeton University. When Madison attended Princeton, the university had recently come under the influence of thinkers from the Scottish Enlightenment. According to A. E. Dick

Howard, "the general thrust" of Scottish philosophy "was an appeal to 'common sense,' a belief that all humans possess an innate sense that enables them to distinguish between good and bad, truth and falsehood, beauty and ugliness" (1985: 22). "Common sense" was common not in the negative sense of "ordinary" as opposed to superior or refined, but in the sense of being universal as opposed to restricted to a privileged few. That is, the Scottish philosophers were asserting that the ability to discern morality, truth, and beauty was not the sole province of a cultural, political, or religious elite, but that all humans are equally endowed with *conscience*, the ability to make reasonable assessments in questions of politics, religion, ethics, and aesthetics.[4]

From this fundamental premise, it was a short step to the principle of religious freedom. To prevent the free exercise of religion—as well as to prevent the free exchange of political viewpoints, debate over scientific laws, and so on—amounted to a restriction of individuals' capacity for moral, spiritual, and intellectual growth. Furthermore, because the freedom of conscience was inalienable, attempts to enforce orthodoxy were futile. No physical coercion could change the fact that individuals would harbor differing opinions about such matters, so attempts to enforce orthodoxy could lead only to hypocrisy—forcing people to confess belief in ideas they disagreed with—and "meanness," or prejudice against those whose conscience led them to beliefs that differed from those of the majority. Religion was an expression of a free conscience, and recognition of this fact led inevitably to the principle of religious liberty.

Madison's thinking about conscience and the freedom of religion had a dramatic influence on the Virginia State Constitution. As an elected representative to the Revolutionary Convention in Virginia, Madison was appointed to a committee to draft a declaration of rights in 1776. George Mason headed the committee, and Mason was the primary author of the declaration. However, it was Madison's influence that most shaped the article on religious liberty. Mason's proposal, after asserting that conscience was the sole and proper guide in matters of religion, declared that "that all Men should enjoy the fullest *Toleration* in the Exercise of Religion" (reprinted in Alley 1985: 51; emphasis added). Madison objected to the concept of toleration and urged that the wording of the article be changed to declare the more radical principle of religious liberty. He also argued that religious liberty was impossible under conditions of religious establishment and thus offered wording that would have had the effect of disestablishing the Episcopal Church:

> That Religion or the duty we owe to our Creator, and the manner of discharging it, being under the direction of reason and conviction only, not of violence or compulsion, all men are equally entitled to the full and free exercise of it according to the dictates of Conscience; and therefore that no man or class of men ought, on account of religion to be invested with peculiar emoluments or privileges; nor subjected to any penalties or disabilities unless under & c. (Reprinted in Alley 1985: 52)

It soon became clear that the goal of disestablishing religion in the state of Virginia would not be achieved at that time, so Madison conceded the point. He and Mason were also unsuccessful in their attempt to define the narrow conditions under which civil government might properly intervene in religious affairs, a clause that foreshadows the Sherbert and Lemon tests that would become the rule of church-state jurisprudence almost two hundred years later.[5] Both Mason's and Madison's proposals asserted the right to exercise religion according to the dictates of conscience "unless under color of Religion, any Man disturb the Peace, the Happiness, or Safety of Society, or of Individuals" or, in Madison's proposal, "unless the preservation of equal liberty and the existence of the state are manifestly endangered" (reprinted in Alley 1985: 51–52).

However, in the Virginia Declaration Madison *was* successful in institutionalizing his understanding of the philosophical basis of religious liberty. In language that clearly expresses the idea that religious freedom is the natural derivative of the inherent freedom of conscience described above, the Virginia Convention adopted the following article on religion in the Declaration of Rights:

> That religion, or the duty which we owe to our creator, and the manner of discharging it, can be directed only by reason and conviction, not by force or violence; and therefore, that all men are equally entitled to the free exercise of religion, according to

the dictates of conscience; and that it is the mutual duty of all to practice Christian forbearance, love, and charity, towards each other. (Reprinted in Alley 1985: 52)

Madison fully realized the limits of what he and Mason had accomplished in the Declaration of Rights. Religious establishments were inherently at odds with the ideal of religious liberty when religious liberty was understood to derive from the inalienable freedom of conscience because the free exercise of conscience depended on the free exchange of ideas and opinions. Religious establishments privileged some religious opinions and ideas and tended toward the repression of others. However, having institutionalized the radical principle of religious liberty as a fundamental basis of Virginia's constitution, Madison had set in motion a process of expanding religious freedom that would lead eventually to the disestablishment of religion in that state.

From Free Exercise to Disestablishment

Experience revealed the flaws in the Virginia Declaration of Rights, but it took nearly ten years before the limits of the protection afforded by the Declaration would be revealed to the public mind. In 1779, only three years after the Declaration of Rights was passed, Jefferson introduced a bill that would have carried the principle of religious freedom to its logical conclusion, disestablishment of the Episcopal Church. Jefferson's Bill for Establishing Religious Freedom, however, failed to gain the support it needed to pass.

The shift in public attitudes toward religious establishments was occasioned five years later, in 1784, when Patrick Henry introduced a bill establishing a provision for teachers of the Christian religion. The bill would have established a tax to support Christian clergy. Individual taxpayers could designate their own churches as beneficiaries, and the taxes of those who made no such designation would go toward the support of public schools. In defense of the bill, Henry argued that it was in keeping with the principle of religious freedom set out in the Declaration of Rights because it did not privilege one sect over another—an argument that has been revived in debates over the First Amendment today, as we will see.

That "nonpreferentialist" argument was further articulated by Richard Henry Lee in a letter to Madison supporting the bill: "The declaration of Rights, it seems to me rather contends against forcing modes of faith and forms of worship, than against compelling contribution for the support of religion in general" (reprinted in Alley 1985: 65). Backed by a powerful faction of Episcopal and Presbyterian clergy, the bill had garnered enough votes to pass.

Madison disagreed with the nonpreferentialist interpretation of the Declaration of Rights and was convinced that the bill ran contrary to popular opinion. He then made what history would record as one of the most brilliant moves of his political career. A gubernatorial election was pending, and Madison and Henry were the only likely candidates. Madison knew that Henry coveted the office and chose not to oppose him in the election. Henry, running unopposed, was thus elected governor. Madison then argued that, with the bill's chief supporter no longer present in the Assembly to speak for the bill, action should be delayed until a public response could be ascertained. Action on the bill was thus deferred until copies of it could be printed and distributed for public comment. The bill's proponents were confident, already having the votes needed for passage, that the bill would pass after the short delay; Madison hoped that the bill would generate a sufficient public outcry to quash it in the next session. During the interim, friends of Madison—who recognized his opponents' bill for what it was, a regressive move away from the progress of religious liberty—persuaded him to write a "memorial" opposing the bill. Thus, Madison set pen to paper and composed his famous "Memorial and Remonstrance," setting out fifteen reasons for opposing state assistance of religion.

The full text of Madison's argument is reproduced in appendix 1, so a summation of his main points will suffice here:

1. (Quoting the Virginia Declaration of Rights, and reiterating the philosophical basis of religious liberty) "Because we hold it for a fundamental and undeniable truth, 'that Religion or the duty which we owe to our Creator and the manner of discharging it, can be directed only by reason and conviction, not by force or violence.' The Religion

then of every man must be left to the conviction and conscience of every man; and it is the right of every man to
exercise it as these may dictate."

2. If religion is an expression of conscience, then it cannot be
subjected to the will of the majority; if religion is exempt
from the collective will, "still less can it be subject to that of
the Legislative Body," which derives its authority from the
collective will. Thus, "Rulers who are guilty of such an encroachment exceed the commission from which they derive
their authority, and are Tyrants," and "People who submit
to it are governed by laws made neither by themselves nor
by an authority derived from them, and are slaves."

3. The bill sets a dangerous precedent, for "Who does not see
that the same authority which can establish Christianity,
in exclusion of all other Religions, may establish with the
same ease any particular sect of Christianity, in exclusion
of all other Sects?"

4. The bill violates the principle of equality before the law,
which guarantees *"equal* title to the free exercise of Religion according to the dictates of Conscience" (emphasis in
the original). We cannot claim a right for ourselves, in
other words, that we are unwilling to extend to others
without violating the principle of equality before the law
because it ceases then to be a claim of right and becomes
a claim of privilege.

5. Worse still, the bill "implies that the Civil Magistrate [i.e.,
a politician] is a competent Judge of Religious Truth."

6. True religion does not need the support of the state. Instead, such support understandably leads people to question the truth of a religion that is unable to stand on its
own merits, but requires coercion for its maintenance.

7. History shows that "establishments, instead of maintaining the purity and efficacy of Religion, have had a contrary operation," leading instead to "pride and indolence
in Clergy, ignorance and servility in the laity, in both
superstition, bigotry, and persecution."

8. History further shows two possible outcomes of religious establishments: Either such establishments "erect

a spiritual tyranny on the ruins of Civil authority" or the establishments become instruments of "political tyranny."

9. &10. Establishments drive away those who love liberty. The policy may seem innocuous enough, but it differs from the Inquisition "only in degree." "The one is the first step, the other the last in the career of intolerance."

11. Establishments lead to competition for power and conflict between religious sects. The experiment in religious liberty "has exhibited proofs that equal and complete liberty, if it does not wholly eradicate [religious discord], sufficiently destroys its malignant influence on the health and prosperity of the State."

12. Establishments are "adverse to the diffusion of the light of Christianity," because the exclusion of non-Christian religions will encourage non-Christian societies to exclude Christianity.

13. The evident injustice of attempts to enforce religious compliance by legal sanctions and the impotence of the state to accomplish this end degrades the authority of the government.

14. Legislation on such an important matter should not be passed without "the clearest evidence" that it enjoys the support of the majority of citizens, and no means of determining that is yet in place.

15. The legislation is at odds with the fundamental basis on which respect for the rights of the people rests. That is, people are endowed with certain inalienable rights, one of which is the free exercise of conscience. If the population allows the state to act in matters of religion, therefore, what is to restrain it from encroaching on others? "Either we must say, that they may control the freedom of the press, may abolish the Trial by Jury, may swallow up the Executive and Judiciary Powers of the State; nay that they may despoil us of our very right of suffrage, . . . or we must say, that they have no authority to enact into law the Bill under consideration."

Madison's argument, in other words, was that recognizing that humans are equally and inalienably endowed with the ability to make reasonable, conscientious judgments about matters of truth led inevitably to the principle of religious free exercise. So too did the principle of religious free exercise lead inevitably to disestablishment. A "nonpreferential" establishment was still an establishment and carried with it the same dangerous tendencies as preferential establishments. Incursions by the state in religious matters—even seemingly minor ones and those that on the surface appeared friendly to religion—could only have the effect of restricting the free exercise of religion because state support of religion narrows the realm established for the free exercise of conscience. The free exercise of conscience, in other words, requires a level playing field on which claims of truth, morality, and beauty may compete on equal terms. The incursion on the freedom of religion might be minor, but it was nonetheless a regressive step, away from the process of expanding liberty set in motion by the Declaration of Rights and toward spiritual tyranny. In "Memorial and Remonstrance," in short, Madison argued explicitly that (1) the free exercise of religion required the disestablishment of religion and (2) disestablishment meant a strict separation of church and state.

Madison's argument against the assessment bill was compelling, and Patrick Henry's proposal to establish a public tax to support religion was soundly defeated in the next session of the Assembly. The counterargument was so compelling, in fact, that shortly thereafter Jefferson's Bill for Establishing Religious Freedom was reintroduced. The bill was signed into law early in 1786, thereby disestablishing religion in the state of Virginia.

In his later years, Madison would reflect on his work to defeat the assessment bill and to expand religious liberty by disestablishing religion in Virginia as one of his proudest accomplishments. He also described Jefferson's bill establishing religious freedom as "the true standard of Religious liberty" and the best expression of its principles "that words can admit" ("Memoranda," reprinted in Alley 1985: 89). Indeed, Jefferson's bill remains one of the most eloquent statements of the philosophical basis of the First Amendment to the U.S. Constitution and is thus worth quoting at some length:

Whereas Almighty God hath created the mind free; that all attempts to influence it by temporal punishments . . . tend only to beget habits of hypocrisy and meanness . . . that the impious presumption of legislators and rulers, civil as well as ecclesiastical, . . . have assumed dominion over the faith of others, setting up their own opinions and modes of thinking as the only true and infallible, and as such endeavoring to impose them on others, hath established and maintained false religions over the greater part of the world, and through all time; that to compel a man to furnish contributions of money for the propagation of opinions which he disbelieves, is sinful and tyrannical; . . . that our civil rights have no dependence on our religious opinions, and to restrain the profession or propagation of principles on supposition of their ill tendency, is a dangerous fallacy, which at once destroys all religious liberty, because he being of course the judge of that tendency will make his opinions the rule of judgment; . . . that it is time enough for the rightful purposes of civil government, for its officers to interfere when principles break out into overt acts against peace and good order; and finally, that truth is great and will prevail if left to herself, that she is the proper and sufficient antagonist to error, and has nothing to fear from the conflict, unless by human interposition disarmed of her natural weapons, free argument and debate, errors ceasing to be dangerous when it is permitted freely to contradict them.[6]

Toward the First Amendment

There is almost universal consensus among First Amendment scholars that the three documents discussed above—the Virginia Declaration of Rights, Madison's "Memorial and Remonstrance," and Jefferson's "Bill for Establishing Religious Freedom"— formed the philosophical basis of the First Amendment to the U.S. Constitution. Ironically, there was a role reversal when it came to the question of a *national* bill of rights. Madison, who had opposed Patrick Henry's proposal and instead fought for and won provisions in the Virginia constitution to protect religious freedom, thought a bill of rights unnecessary in the federal constitution; Patrick Henry, on the other hand, who had sponsored a law benefiting Virginia's religious establishment, now opposed ratification of the Constitution, in part, on the grounds that it afforded insufficient protection for religious liberty.

The concern of opponents of ratification, of course, was not really about religious liberty, but states' rights. The Constitution of 1789 had been devised to give the national government greater sovereignty and thus to correct the weaknesses of the Articles of Confederation. The Articles of Confederation treated the respective states, more or less, as independent, sovereign nations, leaving the federal government powerless to answer problems that arose between the states.[7] The new Constitution answered this problem by vesting in the national government the powers to make treaties, regulate interstate commerce, and adjudicate conflicts between the states, among other things.

Madison's concern for rights was about individual rights not state rights, and he did not see how a national government constituted of enumerated powers could harm individual rights. The federal government only had the authority to act on matters in which the state governments had given up a part of their sovereignty to the federal government, and individual liberties was not among them. Under the new constitution, in Madison's thinking, the protection of individual rights remained a matter of concern for the state governments. If the federal government attempted to legislate on religion, the states would surely rise up to oppose the usurpation of power.

In fact, this is the very tactic that Madison and Jefferson later used to oppose the Alien and Sedition Acts. These acts were passed by the Congress in 1798, allegedly in response to threats by French revolutionaries residing in the United States. In reality, the acts were designed to silence dissent against the Federalist-controlled national government, especially dissent by Jefferson's Republican Party, which advocated American support for the French Revolution and relied heavily on new immigrant votes. The Alien Acts increased the amount of time required for naturalization to fifteen years, which prevented recent immigrants from voting and empowered the federal government to detain and deport unnaturalized "aliens" suspected of subversive activity. The Sedition Act in effect undermined the First Amendment guarantees of free speech and the freedom of the press by making it illegal to rouse opposition to the policies of the federal government. Jefferson and Madison attempted to organize opposition to the acts by the states. They succeeded in passing the Kentucky and Virginia Resolutions, which condemned the Alien and Sedition Acts as an unconstitutional usurpation of power by the federal government. These resolutions did much to unify the nascent Republican Party and to secure its victory in the elections of 1800, when Thomas Jefferson was elected president of the United States.

To Madison, responsibility for the protection of individual liberties lay with the states. However, this fact also concerned him. Not all of the states had achieved the constitutional protections of liberty that Virginia had, and in those that did have declarations of rights, the rights had been honored more in the breech than in the observance. The relatively firm protections for conscience and religious liberty that had been established in Virginia required constant vigilance to maintain because factional interests easily swayed the passions of the public. And this, to Madison, was where the real threat to liberty lay. Writing to Jefferson about the idea of a federal bill of rights in 1788, Madison reflected:

[E]xperience proves the inefficacy of a bill of rights on those occasions when its control is most needed. Repeated violations of these parchment barriers have been committed by overbearing majorities in every State. In Virginia I have seen the bill of rights violated in every instance where it has been opposed to a popular current. Notwithstanding the explicit provision contained in that instrument for the rights of Conscience it is well known that a religious establishment would have taken place in that State, if the legislative majority had found as they expected, a majority of the people in favor of the measure; and I am persuaded that if a majority of the people were now of one sect, the measure would still take place and on narrower ground than was then proposed, notwithstanding the additional obstacle which the law has since created.[8] Whereever the real power in a Government lies, there is the danger of oppression. In our Governments the real power lies in the majority of the Community, and the invasion of private rights is chiefly to be apprehended, not from acts of Government contrary to the sense of its constituents, but from acts in which the Government is the mere instrument of the major number of the constituents. (Reprinted in Alley 1985: 72–73)

If the federal government were to have any power to protect individuals against such infringements, it would have to be endowed with the power to prevent state governments from acting against the rights of the people. In other words, the power for the federal government to protect individual rights would necessarily come at further expense to state sovereignty.

Madison, of course, was eventually convinced of the desirability of amending the Constitution to include a bill of rights. However, when, during the process of composing the Bill of Rights, he introduced a clause that would have empowered the federal government to intervene when state governments infringed on the freedom of conscience, the provision was killed by the very people who had opposed the Constitution on the grounds that it failed to protect the rights of the people. The clause read: "No state shall infringe the equal rights of conscience, nor the freedom of speech, or of the press, nor of the right of trial by jury in criminal cases" (congressional record of Madison's remarks on constitutional amendments, reprinted in Alley 1985: 75–76). The congressional record of Madison's remarks on the proposed constitutional amendments reveals his disappointment: "Mr. Madison conceived this to be the most valuable amendment on the whole list; if there was any reason to restrain the government of the United States from infringing upon these essential rights, it was equally necessary that they should be secured against the state governments; he thought that if they provided against the one; it was an necessary to provide against the other" (reprinted in Alley 1985: 76). No wonder that, after the whole business of composing and ratifying the Bill of Rights was over, Madison described it as a "nauseous project" (Hutson 1991: 69). They had succeeded in passing a bill of rights that prohibited the federal government from doing what it had no power to do and, worse still, had specifically denied the federal government the power it needed to protect the rights of the people against infringement by the states, which was precisely where the power lay to pass legislation touching on individual rights. It would take another sixty years and a civil war before the Constitution would be amended to give the federal government power to intervene against state laws that violated individual rights, and another century before that power was extended to cover matters pertaining to the freedom of religion.

Still, in classic Madison fashion, he understood the value of what he had accomplished in the First Amendment. As had been the case with his work on the Virginia Declaration of Rights, he was unable now to accomplish everything needed to secure religious liberty and protect the right of a free conscience. However, he was able to set in motion a process that had liberty as its logical end. That is, he was able to write the principle of religious liberty into the emerging national culture. He believed that Americans would learn from the experience of states like Virginia and Pennsylvania of the benefits of allowing individuals to exercise conscience freely and thus develop a love of liberty that would sound an alarm when attempts were made to infringe on people's natural and civil rights. In the letter to Jefferson cited above, Madison at first expressed doubt about the efficacy of "parchment barriers." But then, he added, a bill of rights might have two useful purposes:

> 1. The political truths declared in that solemn manner acquire by degrees the character of fundamental maxims of Government, and as they become incorporated with the national sentiment, counteract the impulses of interest and passion.
> 2. Altho' it be generally true . . . that the danger of oppression lies in the interested majorities of the people rather than in usurped actions of Government, yet there may be occasions on which the evil may spring from the latter sources; and on such, a bill of rights will be a good ground for an appeal to the sense of the community. (Reprinted in Alley 1985: 73)

With this background, we can better understand why, during the progress of congressional debates over the First Amendment, Madison expressed little concern about its precise wording, which underwent several revisions before it was passed and presented to the states for ratification. It was not, as some contemporary interpreters of the First Amendment suggest, that Madison envisioned different principles concerning religious freedom and disestablishment for the federal government than he had for the state of Virginia, that while advocating a strict separation of church and state in Virginia, he agreed to nonpreferentialist compromise at the national level.[9] Rather, the First Amendment must be viewed as the logical conclusion of Madison's earlier thinking. As he argued in his "Memorial and Remonstrance," religion was an expression of conscience. As an expression of conscience, the free exercise of religion was an inalienable individual right and could not be subjected to the popular vote. Because the states derived their authority from the popular will, they were, by definition, not authorized to legislate on matters of religion; religious establishments in any form thus inherently represented an usurpation of power. If the state governments could not, in Madison's thinking, justifiably pass laws establishing religion or restricting the free exercise of conscience, still less could the federal government do so whose powers were derived from the states.

The First Amendment, therefore, only reaffirmed what Madison understood already to be the case, which was that the federal government was powerless over conscience and lacked the authority therefore to legislate on matters of conscience. The challenge for securing religious liberty lay not in restricting the powers of the federal government but in restricting the power of the state governments. Three of the states maintained religious establishments into the nineteenth century, and under the terms of the U.S. Constitution as amended in 1791 to include the Bill of Rights, the federal government was powerless to intervene to protect the rights of religious minorities. Still, a national culture of respect for religious liberty began to emerge. Indeed, it was the *ethic* of the First Amendment, not a trial of the First Amendment in federal courts, that eventually led those states that maintained religious establishments to disestablish them. All of the states had dismantled their religious establishments decades before the Fourteenth Amendment, ratified in 1868, empowered the federal government to intervene in cases where state legislation violated individual rights.

Madison greeted each new step in the progress of religious liberty with enthusiasm and expressed disappointment whenever he saw the state meddling in religious affairs. As president, he vetoed acts concerning the incorporation of religious organizations and providing relief to clergy on the grounds that such acts violated the Establishment Clause of the First Amendment. Although as president he took no action against the use of federal money to pay congressional chaplains, chaplains in the armed forces, and the practice of designating national days of prayer and thanksgiving, his private letters show that he objected to these practices in principle. Madison, undeniably, advocated a strict separation of church and state. Although he recognized that a perfect separation of church and state had not yet been achieved, in his retirement he remained hopeful that time and experience would lead the nation toward that end:

> [I]n some parts of our Country, there remains . . . bias towards the old error, that without some sort of alliance or coalition between Government & Religion neither can be duly supported. Such indeed is the tendency to such a coalition, and such its corrupting influence on both parties, that the danger cannot be too carefully guarded against. And in a Government of opinion, like ours, the only effectual guard must be found in the soundness and stability of the general opinion on the subject. Every new & successful example therefore of a perfect separation between ecclesiastical and civic matters is of importance. . . . We are teaching the World the great truth that Governments do better without Kings & Nobles than with them. The merit will be doubled by the other lesson that Religion flourishes in greater purity, without than with the aid of Government. (Letter to Edward Livingston, 1822; reprinted in Alley 1985: 82)

A Broad Interpretation of the First Amendment

We have shown that, for Madison at least, the Bill of Rights and certainly the First Amendment were not finished projects. These were starting points, but the goal of protecting the fundamental rights of the people had yet to be accomplished. The history of the First Amendment shows clearly that Madison did not think his work had accomplished all that was needed to secure the freedom of conscience and thus religious liberty. Instead, he saw his work as setting in motion a process, which had religious liberty as its logical and—he hoped—inevitable end. He would have nodded approvingly at the words of legal scholar Sanford Levinson, quoting Justice Thurgood Marshall:

> "[T]he government they [the Framers] devised was defective from the start." Rectification of those defects "require[ed] several amendments, a civil war, and momentous transformation" before our "system of constitutional government" achieved the "respect for individual freedoms and human rights [that] we hold as fundamental today." (1988: 187)

Those justices today who think that returning to eighteenth-century rules of church-state jurisprudence reflects the "original intent" of the Framers of the Constitution clearly don't know the First Amendment's history. The intention of the author of the First Amendment, and of its eighteenth-century backers, was to set in motion a process of expanding liberty. As Madison's "Memorial and Remonstrance" clearly demonstrates, he would be horrified by contemporary attempts to reverse that process by allowing state sponsorship of religion and by allowing the majority to use the coercive powers of government to restrict religious behavior that poses no threat to public safety.

Madison argued for a broad and expanding understanding of religious liberty. In fact, among his concerns about a national bill of rights was that "some of the most essential rights could not be obtained in the requisite latitude. I am sure that the rights of Conscience in particular, if submitted to public definition would be narrowed much more than they are likely ever to be by an assumed power" (letter to Jefferson, 1788; reprinted in Alley 1985: 72). And responding to a letter from George Eve concerning a bill of rights in 1789, Madison reiterated his support for "satisfactory provisions for all essential rights, particularly the rights of Conscience in the fullest latitude" (reprinted in Alley 1985: 74).

So far in this discussion, we have seen that the freedom of conscience formed the fundamental basis of Madison's ideas about religious liberty, but we must be careful not to imply that the freedom of conscience applies only to religion narrowly conceived. We now argue therefore, more briefly, that just as the recognition of the equal and inalienable right of conscience led Madison to the principle of religious liberty, so too did this understanding form the basis of the freedom of the press, of speech, and of association. Barbara McGraw makes the case for this broad reading of the First Amendment compellingly in her recent book *Rediscovering America's Sacred Ground*. Her analysis is worth quoting at length:

> It was clear to the founders, then, that the necessary conditions that ensure that truth will have an opportunity to prevail include not only free conscience, but also a political context in which the true and the good for individuals and society can arise out of the common debate of a free people where all are permitted to persuade others of their views. . . . [A] review of the language of the First Amendment, itself, and of prior drafts, together with a reading of the record at the time . . . makes clear that the United States Bill of Rights provides the broadest possible scope for free conscience to pursue truth and the goodness that truth engenders. . . . It does so not only by ensuring that individual conscience is free of governmental restraint whatsoever, but also by creating a political context for the expression of free conscience in speech and action through the complimentary rights also granted in the First Amendment . . . , which follow the Religion Clauses. . . . In effect, then, the free speech, free press, assembly, and petition clauses of the First Amendment derive from freedom of conscience. (2003: 85–86)

Indeed, there is some reason to believe that, in the public mind at least, there was greater concern about freedom of political conscience than religious conscience. Consider the following excerpt from "A Receipt [recipe] for an Anti-Federalist Essay," published in *The Pennsylvania Gazette* in November 1787:

> WELL-BORN, nine times—*Aristocracy*, eighteen times—*Liberty of the Press*, thirteen times repeated—*Liberty of Conscience*, once—*Negro slavery*, once mentioned—*Trial by Jury*, seven times—*Great Men*, six times repeated . . . put them altogether, and dish them up at pleasure. (Reprinted in Rutland 1955: 138)

While one must be careful using sarcasm as historical evidence, sarcasm was a favorite mode of political argument in the popular press during the eighteenth century, and the author's meaning, clearly, was that the argument in favor of a bill of rights had become so predictable that one could identify a standard recipe. If that is the case, then the "Receipt for an Anti-Federalist Essay" suggests that what advocates of a bill of rights feared most was that, without specific protection in a bill of rights, the new federal government could stifle *political dissent* by restricting the freedom of the press. The essayist accounted liberty of the press to be mentioned thirteen times in a typical anti-Federalist argument, while freedom of conscience (religion) is accounted only once.

Perhaps the primacy of concern for freedom of the press is made less surprising when one considers that it was mainly in the free press that the debate over ratification of the Constitution then raged. Both supporters and opponents of the Constitution used the free press to publicize their cases, often in the form of opinion essays and pamphlets, which were widely distributed during the ratification process. Probably the most famous example is *The Federalist Papers*, written by Alexander Hamilton, James Madison, and John Jay.

Responding to a complaint by the French ambassador to the United States that he was being abused in the press only a few years after ratification of the Bill of Rights, Chief Justice John Marshall replied that freedom of the press was among America's most sacred values:

> The genius of the Constitution, and the opinions of the people of the United States, cannot be overruled by those who administer the Government. . . . [A]mong those sacred rights considered as forming the bulwark of their liberty, which the Government contemplates with awful reverence . . . there is no one of which the importance is more deeply impressed on the public mind than the liberty of the press. (Quoted in Rogge 1960: 20)

Indeed, Madison himself argued that the scope of this freedom extended even to subversive opinions. Responding to the Sedition Acts of 1798, Madison composed an *Address of the General Assembly to the People of the Commonwealth of Virginia* and a *Report* that defended the *Address* on these First Amendment grounds:

Some degree of abuse is inseparable from the proper use of everything, and in no instance is this more true than in that of the press. It has accordingly been decided by the practice of the states that it is better to leave a few of its noxious branches to their luxurious growth, than, by pruning them away, to injure the vigor of those yielding the proper fruits. And can the wisdom of this policy be doubted by any who reflect that to the press alone, chequered as it is with abuses, the world is indebted for all the triumphs which have been gained by reason and humanity over error and oppression; who reflect that to the same beneficent source the United States owe much of the lights which conducted them to the ranks of a free and independent nation, and which have improved their political system into a shape so auspicious to their happiness? (Quoted in Rogge 1960: 20)

And in March 1801, only days after the Alien and Sedition Acts expired, Thomas Jefferson, paraphrasing his own words in the Virginia bill establishing religious freedom, reiterated the point in his first inaugural address:

If there be any among us who would wish to dissolve this Union or to change its republican form, let them stand undisturbed as monuments of the safety with which error of opinion may be tolerated where reason is left free to combat it. (Quoted in Rogge 1960: 25)

In no uncertain terms, these Founders were saying that dissent was the means by which truth and error are revealed—in civil as well as in religious matters—and conscientious dissent was what they believed to be protected by the First Amendment.

The "freedom of conscience," therefore, is not merely another way of talking about the "freedom of religion," as "religion" is conventionally understood. The freedom of conscience, rather, is the source from which the freedoms of religion, speech, the press, and association are derived. Indeed, without the freedom of conscience—the freedom of the individual to decide for him- or herself questions of morality, truth, and beauty—the First Amendment protections would amount to little more than pleasant words.

Conclusion

Dissenting in a 1985 case concerning "moments of silence" in public schools (*Wallace v. Jaffree*), Chief Justice William Rehnquist called on the Court to abandon its entire approach to the Establishment Clause on the grounds that the history of the First Amendment shows that the Founders intended to prohibit a national church, not to require a strict separation of church and state. Instead, he argued, the Founders intended only to prevent laws that prefer one religion or sect over others, but not to prevent the government from supporting religion over irreligion. He wrote:

> The Framers intended the Establishment Clause to prohibit the designation of any church as a "national" one. The clause was also designed to stop the Federal Government from asserting a preference for one religious denomination or sect over others. . . . As its history abundantly shows, however, nothing in the Establishment Clause requires government to be strictly neutral between religion and irreligion, nor does that clause prohibit Congress or the States from pursuing legitimate secular ends through nondiscriminatory sectarian means.

Rehnquist arrives at this conclusion from a very narrow reading of the congressional debates over the wording on the First Amendment and invokes James Madison as the authority for his interpretation. We leave it to the readers to judge for themselves, but we are left with a strong suspicion either that Justice Rehnquist doesn't know his history or, if he does—alarmingly—that his position on church-state issues is so clouded by ideology that he is willing to rewrite history "from the bench." He is either woefully or willfully ignorant of the philosophical basis of the First Amendment. Neither is acceptable in a justice of the U.S. Supreme Court.

Madison envisioned a broad and expanding scope for the free exercise of conscience. The inalienable freedom of conscience led, in Madison's mind, inevitably to the freedom of religion, the press, speech, and association; and these freedoms led inevitably to the conclusion that government should be power-less to meddle in these affairs. Madison consistently objected to any form of government support for religion because the free exercise of conscience requires a realm of discourse free from the coercive powers of the state. Any attempt by the state to privilege or disadvantage particular opinions—secular or religious—violated the freedom of conscience and was therefore to be strictly avoided. Furthermore, because the First Amendment freedoms derive from the inalienable freedom of conscience, any form of government action in these areas was, by definition, an usurpation of power. The government's power was constituted of those freedoms of which the citizens and states had voluntarily divested themselves. Conscience, being inalienable, and religion, being an expression of conscience, were wholly beyond the scope of legislative authority.

Rehnquist further argued in his dissent that the intentions of the Framers should remain the rule of law today: "As drafters of our Bill of Rights, the Framers inscribed the principles that control today. Any deviation from their intentions frustrates the permanence of that Charter." Should contemporary law be bound by eighteenth-century legislative rhetoric? Would the founders of our nation have desired as much? We sincerely doubt it. They were careful to avoid the possibility of tyranny, whether it was exercised by an individual despot, a privileged few, or by the majority against minorities. We strongly suspect that they would object equally to the tyranny of history.

In any case, as we have seen in this and the previous chapter, Rehnquist's assertion could not be further from the intentions of the Founders. An evolving understanding of rights, as shown in the previous chapter, was written into the Bill of Rights itself, and the freedom of conscience was understood to be the driving force behind its evolution. Madison was fully aware that the First Amendment did not accomplish everything necessary for the protection of fundamental rights and the preservation of liberty. His hope for religious freedom in the newly constituted nation lay, as it had in Virginia, not in "parchment barriers," but in a still-emerging national culture of respect for rights, grounded on and propelled by the freedom of conscience. He hoped, in other words, that the First Amendment, while it did not establish perfect liberty, would set in motion a process of expanding liberty.

There were, certainly, those among Madison's fellows who argued for a narrower interpretation of the ideal of religious liberty. There were those, like Patrick Henry and Richard Henry Lee, who explicitly argued for a nonpreferential church-state system. Madison consistently argued against them. He upheld the ideal of a society in which individuals would enjoy the full freedom to exercise conscience in religious matters and held that "the rights of Conscience . . . [are] more or less invaded by all religious Establishments" (letter to Jasper Adams, 1833; reprinted in Alley 1985: 87). He thus objected to those vestiges of establishment that remained in the United States as an "aberration from the sacred principle of religious liberty" ("Memoranda"; reprinted in Alley 1985: 89). And, we contend, history proves that Madison's was the superior wisdom.

Notes

1. There are several excellent collections of these historical documents. Readers who wish to learn more about the subject of this chapter, or who are critical of our interpretation of the meaning and intent of the First Amendment, may wish to consult Alley, *James Madison on Religious Liberty* (1985); Schwartz, *The Bill of Rights: A Documentary History* (1971); Wilson and Drakeman, *Church and State in American History: Key Documents, Decisions, and Commentary from the Past Three Centuries* (2003); Hamilton, Madison, & Jay, *The Federalist* (1961). The Avalon Project at Yale Law School also has an extensive collection of these historical documents online at www.yale.edu/lawweb/avalon/avalon.htm.

2. Here and elsewhere, we have taken the liberty to correct grammatical errors and to spell out full words where abbreviations appear in the original.

3. Because, as noted earlier, these texts leave room for interpretation, we have quoted liberally from the primary sources in this chapter, so that readers may judge their meaning for themselves. We have also seen fit to reproduce in their entirety two documents universally rec-

ognized to have most influenced the First Amendment: Madison's "Memorial and Remonstrance" and Jefferson's "Act for Establishing Religious Freedom." These are contained in appendix 1.

4. We hardly need to point out the significance of the assertion of intellectual, moral, and aesthetic equality to popular democracy in the United States.

5. See chapter 5.

6. For the full text, see appendix 1.

7. Conservatives today argue that this is the relationship intended by the Constitution. Such "federalism" privileges the sovereignty of the states over the national government; the national government becomes merely a federation of sovereign states. "Federalism" today represents, therefore, an attempt to regress to the system of government devised under the Articles of Confederation, whose flaws the Constitution was designed to remedy.

8. Reference is to the passage of Jefferson's bill for establishing religious freedom.

9. Justice Rehnquist, in the 1985 dissent discussed in the conclusion to this chapter, makes this very argument. He says that the James Madison speaking on behalf of the First Amendment in the U.S. House of Representatives was "speaking as an advocate of sensible legislative compromise, not as an advocate of incorporating the Virginia Statutes of Religious Liberty into the United States Constitution" (*Wallace v. Jaffree*, 1985).

3

The Nineteenth-Century Supreme Court and "Republican Protestantism"

We have argued thus far that, contrary to what Chief Justice Rehnquist and others have claimed, the Framers—or the prime movers among them, like Madison—had a rather expansive vision of the rights of conscience, which included but was not limited to religion. Influential as this understanding of religious liberty might have been to the drafting of the First Amendment, however, historical circumstances of the nineteenth century retarded the expansion of liberty that the First Amendment had set in motion and led, at the Supreme Court, to a church-state perspective quite at odds with the Framers' perspective.

In this chapter, we argue that the line of argumentation followed by today's regressive justices is more in keeping with post-ratification, *nineteenth*-century Supreme Court theorists than the *eighteenth*-century constitutional authors they continually invoke. It was those nineteenth-century jurists who laid the foundation for the argument that conscience necessarily meant religion (and that religion meant Christianity). And it was those jurists—and not the Constitution's authors—who implemented this worldview in the earliest of "church-state" decisions, which are so often cited by today's nonpreferentialists—those who would lower the wall of separation in order to "accommodate" religion.

Regardless of the Framers' rhetorical energy that went into shaping initial conceptions of the freedoms envisioned in the First Amendment, the Supreme Court itself was silent on the matter for decades. Well into the nineteenth century—indeed, almost to that century's end—the Court's few proclamations on the subject seemed to provide ample evidence that the adoption of the First Amendment had completely "settled" the religious liberty question for which it had been written. But although it may at first blush seem as if the Court was absent from the discussion of the First Amendment, it is more accurately the case that the Court—and more specifically, certain of its members—was developing positions on religion and religious institutions that would provide the foundations for later First Amendment jurisprudence, if not in the ways in which we have come to expect them today. Throughout the nineteenth century, the Court was, in fact, quite vocal about matters related to religion and its shape and place in a democratic society. As we shall see, by the end of the nineteenth century—and even into the early years of the twentieth—while the Supreme Court *seemed* to be silent on the conceptions of religious liberty embodied in the First Amendment, it was in fact establishing a position on religion in society entirely reflective of the environment in which it operated. The Court's early attitude toward religion—and thus, its position on the First Amendment—was more a product of its own institutional development and the nineteenth-century Protestant culture in which it developed than of any larger philosophical notions of religious liberty.

The Religious Climate of the Early Republic

We may be doing the Court a disservice if we attempt to apply the urgency of the question about religious freedom that we feel today to those early years of the Republic. This is not to argue that the matter was unimportant—as we have noted, questions related to religion and religious liberty were of the greatest importance then—but only that it was framed by the Court within an entirely different context. The larger issue of federalism—the relationship between the national government and the states—served as the backdrop upon which any theory regarding government's relationship to religion was placed. As we will see,

Christianity would become one of the federalist tools of nation-alization—states could regulate the behavior of religious communities, but the national government would develop its citizenship by leveling the field religiously. That is, individuals could believe as their consciences dictated but they had to conform to specific behavioral norms as citizens of the state. The religion issues were not unimportant, but they fit into a larger debate over the negotiation of political power.

It is therefore a healthy historical corrective—particularly given the eloquence surrounding the religion clauses of the First Amendment (see Miller 1988)—to remember that what today is the First Amendment was actually the third (of twelve) sent to the states for adoption. The first on the list (addressing apportionment) was rejected, while the second (addressing the timing of salary increases for members of Congress) was ratified in 1992 to become the Twenty-Seventh Amendment. Religion was third on the list of what would be the Bill of Rights, behind two amendments of seemingly greater concern to the drafting body. Federalism and its subsequent needs (formulas for representation, salaries for its representatives) were of greater concern than the rights of those being served—at least, to the majority of those drafting the document, if not to the citizens of the states ratifying it.

This corrective is even more effective when we recall a point raised often by scholars who have argued that the Framers had no intention of creating a strict separation of religion and government when they fashioned what we now know as the First Amendment. This point—that Congress approved funds to pay for a congressional chaplain on the same day they debated the language of what would become the First Amendment (see *Marsh v. Chambers*, 1983)—may not be as conclusive in the argument for a nonpreferentialist position toward church-state relations as some might think. In part because of migration patterns into the colonies, and in part because of the British legacy in those colonies, religion and society were not nearly as distinctly separated as they seem today, making assumptions about religion, and sensitivities to diversity, entirely different from what we might assume. Most citizens were Christian, and—given

both the relatively small Catholic population and the institutionalized anti-Catholicism in the colonies and early Republic—
most of those Christians were Protestant. Religious communities
with which we are now familiar—and who, for the last forty
years, have been regular participants in the debate over the
meaning and limits of religious freedom—either were not present in significant numbers in the early Republic (for examples,
Jews), or did not even exist at the time (for example, Jehovah's
Witnesses, Seventh-Day Adventists, or Mormons). In his examination of the religious traditions represented in the ratification
conventions around the states, historian Stephen Marini uncov-
ers an amazing homogeneity; there was certainly a diversity of
Protestant traditions represented in those conventions, but few
Catholics, significantly fewer Jews (if any), and not much else
(1994). This homogeneity explains much about the early Republic: not only the shape of the laws, which reflected a Protestant
bias, but also the nature of the debates, which seemed unconcerned about the rights of religious minorities as we understand
them today, but certainly concerned about the powers of diverse
Protestant religious communities, who were unequally vested in
the powers of state.

It is this kind of assumption of relative cultural homogeneity—
still common enough in some minds—that set the tone for the early
Republic. Often referred to as "Republican Protestantism," this attitude was based on the notion not only that Protestant Christianity
was the only tradition represented in society, and not only was it the
only one worth being represented in society, but also that it was the
only one with the wherewithal to build, improve, and maintain that
society. It is therefore not surprising that, within certain parameters,
laws and customs would reflect a generally Christian—if not a
specifically Protestant—worldview. Historian Robert Handy, in his
analysis of American religious history through the nineteenth century, describes a world in which all public institutions were made
to look like the dominant community within that culture (1984; see
also Lippy 1978). It is not devious, it is not malicious—it is, in fact,
both human nature and easily understood—and it certainly explains comments like those of Chief Justice John Marshall who,
early in the nineteenth century, wrote:

The American population is entirely Christian, and with us, Christianity and Religion are identified. It would be strange, indeed, if with such a people, our institutions did not presuppose Christianity, and did not often refer to it, and exhibit relations to it. Legislation on the subject is admitted to require great delicacy because freedom of conscience and respect for our religion both claim our most serious regard. (Quoted in Adams and Emmerich 1990: 27–28)

It also explains the position of those throughout the nineteenth century who, despite arguments to the contrary, understood the U.S. Constitution as a Christian document, pointing to its use of the Christian dating system (Article VII: " . . . Year of Our Lord . . .") and its treatment of Sundays (Article I, section 7, which does not count Sundays among the days between when a bill is passed and when it can become law without the president's signature) as proof that, at the very least, it reflected the Christian assumptions of the people it governed (Dreisbach 1996). Common enough among the citizenry—but probably reinforced by demographics in the early Republic's white, male, land-owning leadership—was the notion that this was a Christian commonwealth, founded by Christians, maintained by Christians, and only gracious ("tolerant") to non-Christians as long as they acted relatively Christian. Even Madison's groundbreaking work on the Virginia Declaration of Rights, which we discussed in the previous chapter, retained the imperative "that it is the mutual duty of all to practice Christian forbearance, love, and charity, towards each other." Not all *Christians*, but all *people*, were expected to practice "Christian forbearance." Blasphemy prosecutions, Sunday closing laws, Bible readings (and, more to the point, punishment not just for refusing to read the King James Version (KJV) but also for requesting a nonauthorized— that is, non-KJV—translation), and most especially voting and candidacy restrictions seemed able to maintain in the states what the federal Constitution prohibited on the national level (see Borden 1984; Way 1987; J. K. Wilson 1990).

That this "Republican Protestantism" was also a manifestation of federalism—the states could, and did, maintain religious establishments and religious restrictions even after the adoption of the federal Constitution—is yet another reminder that the drafting of the First Amendment did not signal an immediate wave of enlightenment toward religious liberty, but may be better understood as a political calculation. Historian of American religion John F. Wilson argues that the First Amendment was written the way that it was so that the states would not fear the interference of the federal government, and—more to the point— would not be suspicious of any designs by other states dominated by different religious traditions to compromise each others' preferred religious institutions (1990). Those seeking to protect Congregationalist establishments in the North would not be willing to ratify a constitution if they believed that those seeking to protect Episcopalian establishments in the South were going to control the government. By leaving the federal government out of the business of religion, while permitting the states to maintain their status quo, the Framers avoided almost certain failure in the ratification process. In other words, in order to safeguard the ratification of the newly drafted U.S. Constitution, the Framers minimized one of the more contentious elements within it—religious institutions and their protection by the states.

Thus it was not that religion was not an issue, but that, with significantly fewer players in the arena, the terms of the debate were significantly different; the players that there were therefore understood the debate from an entirely different perspective. For more than the first one hundred years of the Court's history, its understanding of the world—and more specifically, the First Amendment—would be shaped by a heavily Protestant worldview. And it is this perspective that we have to adopt if we are to understand the development of the Court's early attitudes toward religion.

The Early Court and the Story "Story"

As we noted earlier, because it was a "given," this Protestant worldview seemed to have minimal direct effect on the Court's interpretation of the First Amendment. And to no one's surprise, there was a minimum of activity in that area for most of the nineteenth century. In fact, only once between 1789 and 1878 did the Court rely on that amendment's religion clauses, and that was only to affirm the principles of federalism by refusing to get involved—the amendment clearly said "Congress shall make no law," so any conflict based on a state's actions were not in the federal court's jurisdiction (*Permoli v. New Orleans*, 1845).

In part this was because of the relatively narrow worldview provided by Republican Protestantism, and in part it was because the rather blissful ignorance that was the by-product of cultural arrogance meant that pressing matters of state—matters other than religion—could be attended to without distraction. Not surprisingly, in the first several decades of its existence the Supreme Court was much less concerned with the meaning of religion under the First Amendment and much more concerned with questions of nationalism, federalism, and a definition of its own position within that structure. Supreme Court historian Robert McCloskey argues that from the Judiciary Act of 1789 until the Civil War, "the dominant interest of the Supreme Court was in the greatest of all questions left unsolved by the Founders—the nation-state relationship" (1960: 28). Decisions during these early years, but particularly during the early years of the Marshall Court (1801–1835), tended to focus on the power of the Court to review (and even overturn) congressional legislation (*Marbury v. Madison*, 1803), state legislation (*Fletcher v. Peck*, 1810), or decisions of state courts (*Martin v. Hunter's Lessees*, 1816).

This makes perfect sense, not only from a political point of view but also from an institutional one. On the one hand, regardless of the particular politics of the justices (Federalist or Republican), those who understood the desire for a strong Supreme Court would also understand the need for a strong federal government, making federalism and judicial supremacy central to the survival of the Court. On the other hand, religion, as important an issue as it might have been to the Framers, did not seem to motivate the early justices of the Supreme Court, who—regardless of the concerns being raised in the state courts (see Way 1987)—were largely able to avoid the questions raised by the

First Amendment and operate as if equating "religion" with Protestant Christianity was sufficient as far as the matter went.

Beyond the confines of the First Amendment, however, there is a wealth of information related to how the Court might have understood religion, and it is here where we see more clearly the reflection of the Protestant worldview. Nearly four dozen times between 1815 and the end of the nineteenth century, the Court announced decisions for cases involving questions related to religion. These decisions rarely made reference to the First Amendment—and for that reason they have been largely overlooked by First Amendment scholars investigating religion—but they do reveal how the Court understood religion and its place in American society.

Justice Joseph Story (1779–1845), who served on the Court from 1811 until his death in 1845, is of particular use to us, not only because of his lengthy career as a justice, author, and teacher of constitutional law, but also because of the impact his work would have during his tenure and for the remainder of the nineteenth century.[1] Identified as "an American Blackstone" (Dunne 1963), compared with England's Lord Coke (Dowd 1965: 648), called one of the top ten most important justices in the history of the Supreme Court (Schwartz 1995)—second, according to the author, behind only Chief Justice John Marshall—and one whose "position in the history of American law is unique" and whose work "must be counted one of the controlling factors in the shaping of American law" (Pound 1914: 678, 693), Story would be one of the most relied upon and most powerful interpreters of the Constitution for the first one hundred years of the Court's operation. Of particular importance for us, however, is Story's role in defining religion and its relationship to government. Of the ten decisions involving questions relating to religion or religious institutions during his three decades on the Court—there was none before him—Story would author more than half. Wrote Story biographer James McClellan, "Not only is Story the only Supreme Court justice who has ever attempted to answer Jefferson" on the issue of Christianity and its relation to the common law, "but he is also the first member of the Court to deliver opinions on the subject of religious freedom in America."

As such, McClellan maintains, his opinions "raise considerable doubts about the constitutional and historical accuracy of the *Everson* and *McCollum* decisions, which ushered in the current doctrines, and of the more recent school prayer and Bible-reading cases of 1962 and 1963" (1971: 119). If this is so, he is certainly worth examining.

Like many of his fellow justices, Story was most concerned with the health and future of the new nation, and he expressed these concerns through the lens of nationalism. Story had been appointed as a Republican justice by a Republican president (Madison), but was known even then to have federalist tendencies. While still an elected official, he had opposed Jefferson's embargo, which adversely raised his profile with that president; Jefferson would later identify Story as a "pseudo-Republican" and recommend against his appointment (Commager 1953: 35). (Madison did, in fact, nominate three others before he nominated Story: the first two—including John Quincy Adams—turned down the opportunity, while the Senate rejected the third. See Konefsky 1988: 1136.) Once on the bench, he understood what other justices had come to understand—that, in order to do its job effectively, a truly Supreme Court needed a strong central government with judicial authority vested in its highest court. One of his earlier decisions, *Martin v. Hunter's Lessees* (1816)—one that historian Henry Steele Commager calls his "first great opinion" (1953: 46)—has been called "one of the most sweeping decisions that Story ever issued concerning the judicial supremacy of the Supreme Court over the states" (Dowd 1965: 652). Subsequent decisions written by Story—like the 1842 decision in *Swift v. Tyson*, which argued for a national commercial law—as well as his treatises, would echo his nationalist tendencies, justifying the label "neo-Federalist" (Dunne 1963: 321).

Unlike the Republican Party with which he had early identified, Story understood the authority of the Constitution as deriving directly from the people, and not from the people via the states. As early as 1816, he would argue in *Martin* that the U.S. Constitution "was ordained and established, not by the states in their sovereign capacities, but emphatically, as the preamble of the constitution declares, by 'the people of the United States'"

(*Martin v. Hunter's Lessees*). By this, it seems, Story meant several things. First, he meant that the states were the creations of the federal government, and not vice versa. Second, he meant that the federal courts—but particularly the Supreme Court—had the authority to interpret the Constitution not only as it applied to congressional action (which was an entirely different battle over the balance of powers), but also as it applied to state law or a state court's decision. As Story understood it, this interpretation of the Constitution and the role of the Court was "not the revolt of a creature against its creators, but the legitimate assertion of a power granted by the sovereign people" (Powell 1985: 1304).

One of Story's most important statements of this notion of nationalism was in his three-volume opus, *Commentaries on the Constitution*, first published in 1833, which Commager identifies as "the Bible of the nationalists" (1953: 53). Written in response to the Nullification movement building in the decades before the Civil War, this treatise

> provided nationalists with a detailed refutation of the histori-
> cal and theoretical underpinnings of the states' rights theory of
> the Constitution, and supplied supporters of an expansive do-
> mestic role for the federal government with a vigorous asser-
> tion of the federal government's powers and responsibilities.
> (Powell 1985: 1293–94)

According to Commager, in the federal courts this treatise "achieved an authoritativeness which rivaled that of the *Federalist Papers* themselves," a privilege they held to the end of the nineteenth century. Commager even suggests that they may have been the foundation for the shift in constitutional structure that would follow the Civil War and become manifest in the Fourteenth Amendment's extension of the federal court's protections of citizens against the states (1953: 55).

The power of Story's argument can be found in the reaction it elicited from those who advocated states' rights (which would also include a number of the more nonpreferentialist justices on today's Court). Indeed, a critique by Abel Upshur, a conservative Virginian who would eventually serve as secretary of the navy and secretary of state under President Tyler, illuminates the power of Story's arguments. Completely uninterested in the justice's interpretation of the religion clauses, Upshur argued that Story was trying "to establish the doctrine, that the Constitution of the United States is a government of 'the people of the United States,' as contradistinguished from the people of the several states; or, in other words, that it is a consolidated, and not a federative system" (Upshur [1840] 1971: 14). Upshur argued that, since the states predated the national government, they were not subordinate to it. The states approved the Constitution; the citizens of the nation did not.

But Story clearly disagreed. The national charter was a reflection of natural law, and as such was the highest statement of truth and reality possible. This could not mean that the states had any greater authority than the federal government; such a position would be unnatural and blasphemous. As a creature of the national charter, the Supreme Court was clearly the only organ with the authority to interpret it. And finally, the Constitution represented a covenant among the people, the government, and (by implication) the forces at work behind the natural law. The states, both as products of that covenant and as lesser entities, could not interfere in that covenant unless given the authority by the parties involved; that is, either by the people or by their representative national government. Just after assuming his seat on the Supreme Court, Story would write: "Let us prevent the possibility of a division, by creating great national interests which shall bind us in an indissoluble chain" (W. Story 1851, i: 254). Religion (and, as we will see, this meant his religion) would be one of the links in that chain.

Justice Story differentiated between general religious attitudes—or, more exactly, general Protestant Christian morality—religious communities, and individual religious conscience. He had no difficulty with the idea that religion was a necessary tool in the administration of society. He applauded what he understood as the history of his native New England, from which he drew a lesson on the value of religion in the creation of a healthy society. He wrote:

> The colonies planted on the continent of North America, were in a great measure the offspring of private adventure and enterprise, and, with a single exception, of the spirit of commerce.

That exception is New-England [sic]; and it is an exception as extraordinary as it is honorable. We [i.e., New Englanders] owe our existence to the love of religion; and I may say, exclusively to the love of religion. (1828: 30)

Religion was the foundation upon which governments built good citizens; therefore, it was worthy of government support. Story dismissed those who criticized his understanding of the universal application of Christianity within the American context:

Now, there will probably be found few persons in this, or any Christian country, who would deliberately contend, that it was unreasonable, or unjust to foster and encourage the Christian religion generally, as a matter of sound policy, as well as of revealed truth. In fact, every American colony . . . did openly, by the whole course of its laws and institutions, support and sustain, in some form, the Christian religion; and almost invariably gave a peculiar sanction to some of its fundamental doctrines. ([1833] 1970, ii: 724)

In other words, the law of each of the colonies was based on Christian principles, and no one would have expected them to be otherwise and to succeed. This unofficial establishment of Christianity was therefore historically grounded and illustrated the meaning of the First Amendment, which was written "not to countenance, much less to advance Mahometanism, or Judaism, or infidelity, by prostrating Christianity." Rather, it was designed "to exclude all rivalry among Christian sects, and to prevent any national ecclesiastical establishment, which should give to an hierarchy the exclusive patronage of the national government" ([1833] 1970, ii: 728). The goal was not the freedom to foster religious diversity, but the avoidance of a "national ecclesiastical establishment," such as the Church of England. He speculated that

at the time of the adoption of the constitution [sic], and of the [First A]mendment to it, now under consideration, the general, if not the universal, sentiment in America was, that Christianity ought to receive encouragement from the state, so far as was not incompatible with the private rights of conscience, and the freedom of religious worship. An attempt to level all religions, and to make it a matter of state policy to hold all in utter indifference, would have created universal disapprobation, if not universal indignation. ([1833] 1970, ii: 726)

Christianity was favored as the moderator of proper behavior, but no specific Christian community was countenanced by the government to the detriment of another. This general application of Christianity kept all groups on an equal political footing, while fostering good citizenship with sound moral training.

This means that, at the very least, Story was clearly opposed to any one religious community enjoying a legally established monopoly on public power. In a speech delivered in 1828, he noted that "[t]he fundamental error of our ancestors, an error which began with the very settlement of the colony, was a doctrine, which has since been happily exploded, I mean the necessity of a union between church and state" (55). Most assuredly, the federal Constitution would not countenance the establishment of a national religious institution—in that sense, "church" was most clearly separated from state. He wrote that the purpose of Article VI (which included prohibitions on religious oaths for federal office) was "to cut off for ever every pretense of any alliance between church and state in the national government" ([1833] 1970, ii: 705). As a means of protecting against the possibility of one religious group dominating others on the national level, the federal government could not show support for a particular sect through the use of a religious test. Story concluded that, "without some prohibition of religious tests, a successful sect, in our country, might, by once possessing power, pass test-laws, which would secure to themselves a monopoly of all the offices of trust and profit, under the national government" ([1833] 1970, ii: 709).

> Thus, the whole power over the subject of religion is left exclusively to the state governments, to be acted upon according to their own sense of justice, and the state constitutions; and the Catholic and the Protestant, the Calvinist and the

Arminian, the Jew and the Infidel, may sit down at the common table of the national councils, without any inquisition into their faiths, or mode of worship. ([1833] 1970, ii: 731)[2]

Given what we know of Story's devotion to nationalism, we might wonder why the states would be permitted to operate in religious matters in ways not permitted on the national level. Part of the reason might come from his understanding of federalism; that is, what is left to the states after the federal government has exerted its power? As he notes in his treatise, "it is impossible for those, who believe in the truth of Christianity, as a divine revelation, to doubt, that it is the especial duty of government to foster, and encourage it among all the citizens and subjects." However, this was not the whole of the matter; he notes that the "real difficulty" was in determining the balance of power—a true federalist concern—both between the national and state government, and between the government and the individual. Regardless of the value of Christianity such that government should "encourage it among all the citizens and subjects," there was still the matter of "the right of private judgment in matters of religion, and of the freedom of public worship according to the dictates of one's conscience" ([1833] 1970, ii: 722). Limitation, not promotion, was the question.

But where to set those limits? Story was a firm believer in the beauty and truth of Christianity and understood it as the model for the highest level of morality, writing that "the influence of Christianity [on the human character] . . . is the most instructive of all speculations, which can employ the intellect of many" (1828: 31). But he also understood the individual believer's right to be wrong. Interpreting the Free Exercise Clause, Story noted that "the duty of supporting religion, and especially the Christian religion, is very different from the right to force the consciences of other men, or to punish them for worshipping God in the manner, which, they believe, their accountability to him requires" ([1833] 1970, ii: 727). He believed that Christianity was "necessary to the support of civil society, and shall ever attend to its institutions and acknowledge its precepts as the pure and natural sources of private and social happiness." But while "[t]he man who could subvert its influence will never receive countenance from me," nonetheless that same man's "ingenuous doubt shall ever be protected as a *misfortune*, but not a *crime*" (W. Story 1851, i: 92; emphasis in the original). "If there is any right," he wrote, "sacred beyond all others, because it imports everlasting consequences, it is the right to worship God according to the dictates of our own consciences" (1828: 45).

In this position, Story revealed his Calvinist background. Although he had converted to Unitarianism in college, and would eventually serve as president of the American Unitarian Association (see Dunne 1963: 325), Story biographer Kent Newmyer suggested that his conversion "did not obliterate all traces of his early Calvinism," and that "traces are found more in his secular intellectual system than in his religion" (Newmyer 1985: 29). Clearly, Story's Calvinist roots informed his notions of conscience.

As Madison had written, religion was "the duty we owe our Creator," and not a matter of personal choice (see "Memorial and Remonstrance"). Conscience, according to Protestant Reformer John Calvin, was not "free" in the sense of being free to choose according to whim. Rather, it was an irresistible force that required the believer's attention; even today, an individual believer may seem like she is choosing to convert from one religious tradition to another, but she will understand it in terms of a necessity to convert—some force within her compels it. For Story, the "freedom" involved was the freedom to pursue this conscientiously required direction and not the "freedom" to sample religious alternatives or to act as one wanted in the face of restrictive legislation. According to Story, the individual's beliefs were "beyond the just reach of any human power. They are given by God, and cannot be encroached upon by human authority, without a criminal disobedience of the precepts of natural, as well as revealed religion" ([1833] 1970, ii: 727). Thus, as one historian would recognize, in Story a strong humanitarian instinct would manifest itself as "an almost militant instinct of religious tolerance"—more like Mason than Madison—that was "unquestionably based on *noblesse oblige* rather than democratic idealism" (Dunne 1963: 327).

But there was still the matter of the states, which not only maintained religious establishments as Story finished his treatise (the last state to "disestablish" was Massachusetts, 1833), but which also continued to control religious behaviors throughout the nineteenth century. Story's understanding, shaped by Calvinist Protestantism and federalism, provides the answer:

> Our fathers had not arrived at the great truth, that *action*, not *opinion*, is the proper object of human legislation; that religious freedom is the birthright of man; that governments have no authority to inflict punishment for conscientious differences of opinion; and that to worship God according to our own belief is not only our privilege, but is our duty, our absolute duty, from which no human tribunal can absolve us. (1828: 47; emphasis in the original)

As a Protestant, Story understood religion to be a matter of belief; Protestants were emphatic in their denunciation of the Catholic doctrine of salvation through "good works." Behaviors were not central to Protestant Christianity, therefore, but beliefs were. Freedom of beliefs—particularly the freedom to believe what the conscience dictated—was what was necessary, and Story's understanding of the federal Constitution protected that. Not only were actions not central to Protestantism, but they were also a possible threat to political stability. Writes scholar of religion and law John Witte of John Adams's involvement in the Massachusetts constitution of 1780 (which placed limitations on non-Christians), "too much religious freedom is an invitation to depravity and license" (Witte 1999: 251–52). The state, therefore, as the creature of the nation, would retain the authority to control behaviors purporting to be religious. And the nation benefited from the unity created and maintained by a good, Christian citizenry.

The Proof in the Pudding

Thus was Story's federalist sense of nationalism preserved, even in his musings on religion. The state could restrict behavior, according to Story, because behaviors were not part of a Protestant understanding of salvation. One was saved by faith and grace, and not by works. The conscience guided the believer to the truth, meaning that consciences needed to be free, and were, in any event, protected by natural law. As such, they were also protected by the national charter, since, Story believed, the Constitution "embodied natural law, and natural law was not a matter of fashion, but of eternal principles" (Commager 1953: 55). However, one's actions, particularly if they migrated into the realm of what society considered misbehavior, could be controlled by the state.

Over the course of the nineteenth century, the Supreme Court would execute in their decision-making Story's conception of religion in American society. As we noted earlier, there were only a few decisions whose logic was based on interpretations of the First Amendment; but in nearly fifty decisions (in cases as varied as contract disputes, probate cases, real estate claims, and inheritance disputes), the Court would bring to its work the "Republican Protestant" vision of religion in society articulated by Story. At least seventeen times during the nineteenth century, the Supreme Court addressed the issue of religion in the form of religious organizations and their relationship to property (real estate, money, or other assets). In the second half of the nineteenth century alone, the Supreme Court would adjudicate matters related to the sanctity of Sunday as the Lord's Day eight times and would affirm states' rights to designate that day as sacred even as it distinguished the activities involved in litigation—from legal business (issuing verdicts or executing contracts, for example) to mundane business (closing barber shops or limiting railroad travel, for example). In that same period of time, it would address issues related to one particular religious tradition—the Church of Jesus Christ of Latter-day Saints, also known as Mormons—no fewer than eighteen times. And across all of these decisions, a pattern emerges reflective of Republican Protestantism. For example, in the church property decisions, the High Court protected the rights of a religious institution against the disestablishment designs of a particular state (*Terrett v. Taylor*, 1815)—Virginia, to be exact—and assigned property rights to municipalities with the understanding that the property be used for purposes in line with religious public service (*Town of Pawlet v. Clark*, 1815). While it ruled that certain activities were not within the meaning of state restrictions on Sunday activities (*Ball v. United States*, 1891; *Stone v. United States*, 1897), it also ruled that states could limit hair-cutting businesses on Sundays (*Petit v. Minnesota*, 1900). And most powerfully, the Court ruled over and over again that Mormons could believe what they wished, but could not act on those beliefs (*Reynolds v. United States*, 1878; *Davis v. Beason*, 1890). Nowhere did it ever suggest that Sunday could not be set aside by the states (only that certain activities were not included in those set-asides); nowhere did it ever suggest that Mormons had a right to engage in unorthodox activities (even if they did claim that they were required to perform such activities because of the demands of conscience). As for issues related to church property, the pattern is a bit more complex: If a religious community was duly incorporated, it had certain corporate rights to property, but if not, the community had certain responsibilities to maintain those religious responsibilities that would have been performed by the church had it been incorporated. But interestingly, if there was a dispute *within* the religious community, that dispute could be resolved by the courts—not just in probate cases, but even at times of sectarian schism and institutional disintegration. In all of these decisions, the Court rendered its decisions in a manner generally reflective of the formula established by Justice Story; religion is necessary for a moral citizenry, Protestant Christianity is the model of religion, and belief is free and protected by natural law (and the Constitution) while actions are not and are within the jurisdiction of the states (which can limit them based on their own locally preferred version of Protestant Christianity).

Two decisions in particular best illustrate the Republican Protestantism in operation at the Supreme Court during the nineteenth century. The first, *Vidal v. Girard's Executors* (1844), was Justice Story's last opinion related to religion issues and may be his strongest statement thereon. More powerfully, there is little doubt that—unlike other work of the Supreme Court—the thoughts contained within it are solely those of the author's; as Story wrote to the Honorable James Kent late in the summer of 1844, "The Court were unanimous, and not a single sentence was altered by my brothers, as I originally drew it" (W. Story 1851, ii: 469). The dispute concerned a sizeable donation left by Stephen Girard to the city of Philadelphia and the Commonwealth of Pennsylvania for a number of different civic improvements, one of which was a school for orphans. The will elaborated on the specifics of the school, stating that "no ecclesiastic, missionary, or minister of any sect whatsoever, shall ever hold or excuse any station or duty whatever in the said college; nor shall any such person ever be admitted for any purpose, or as a visitor, within the premises appropriated to the purpose of said college." The will also stated that no animosity was meant toward religious groups, but that the restriction was intended to keep religious rivalries out of the school and to promote a healthier atmosphere of morality that could provide the students with the foundations needed to select a religious faith once they had reached a more mature status. Girard's family members, contesting the will, argued that, among other things, this restriction against members of the clergy was anti-Christian and therefore violated the laws of Pennsylvania. (The decision quotes the Pennsylvania constitution, which states that "no human authority can in any case whatever control or interfere with the rights of conscience." Tellingly, neither party disputed the fact that Christianity was declared part of the laws of Pennsylvania.)

Justice Story concluded otherwise. He acknowledged, "the Christian religion is part of the common law of Pennsylvania" and noted that there was nothing in the will that was antagonistic toward religion; true Christianity (that is, Protestant Christianity, with its belief in the priesthood of all believers) need not be taught by ministers. Girard's concern and generosity for the orphans proved his genuine Christianity, and his concern for their moral development was enough to convince the Court that there was nothing in the will that violated the laws of Pennsylvania. Philadelphia got its orphanage, and Girard's family got a lesson in Republican Protestantism.

The other representative opinion, *Reynolds v. United States* (1879)—in which the Supreme Court affirmed Congress's constitutional authority to prohibit polygamy—exactly reflects Story's notions of the relationship between Christianity and the American government. As one of us has argued elsewhere, the *Reynolds* decision (and the host of decisions related to the Church of Jesus Christ of Latter-Day Saints and its members) centered as much on competition between the federal government and the leadership of the Church over the rights to control the Utah territory as it did on the clearly mainstream Protestant concerns over the Mormon practice of plural marriage (Mazur 1999). As such, it reflects both of Story's concerns: federalism and the proper place of Christianity in securing the morality of good citizens.

The decision, clearly written by a Court aware of its place in constitutional history, is the first lengthy discussion of the First Amendment. The case involved a Mormon married more than once who was encouraged to test the constitutionality of the Morrill Act of 1862, the first federal statute to prohibit polygamy (a practice primarily of Mormon leadership since at least the 1850s). Chief Justice Waite, writing for the Court, noted "'religion' is not defined in the Constitution," and turns to "the history of the times in the midst of which the provision was adopted" in order "to ascertain its meaning." After reviewing the history of the Virginia statute and the "Memorial and Remonstrance," Chief Justice Waite concluded:

> Congress cannot pass a law for the government of the Territories which shall prohibit the free exercise of religion. The first amendment to the Constitution expressly forbids such legislation. Religious freedom is guaranteed everywhere throughout the United States, so far as congressional interference is concerned. (*Reynolds v. United States*)

However, "the question to be determined," he realized "is, whether the law now under consideration comes within this prohibition." To no one's surprise, it did not. In a statement as reflective of Justice Story as it was of Jefferson and Madison, Chief Justice Waite would utter words that have become the benchmark for all First Amendment decision making since: "Congress was deprived of all legislative power over mere opinion, but was left free to reach actions which were in violation of social duties or subversive of good order" (*Reynolds v. United States*). The federal government could, therefore, limit, or even prohibit, the Mormon practice of plural marriage. (As the action occurred on federal territory, and not in any one state, there was no state with the authority to act.) Justice Story's doctrine of limiting action if not belief became the justification for the first First Amendment decision to take on the religious liberty obligations of the federal government.

This is not to say that Jefferson or Madison did not recognize the authority of the government (federal or state) to control dangerous behavior. Even the Court's description of the Mormon practice—"odious among the northern and western [that is, the Christian] nations of Europe, and, until the establishment of the Mormon Church, . . . almost exclusively a feature of the life of Asiatic and of African [that is, the non-Christian] people"—could be found in some of the Christian-leaning writings of Madison and Jefferson. But the combination of all of these elements—federalism, the split between belief and action, and the privileging of traditional Protestant Christianity as morally superior—point more to the Republican Protestantism that is the hallmark of Justice Story's doctrine than to the Enlightenment writings of Madison and Jefferson.

Because it has become the foundation for much of contemporary church-state doctrine—particularly with the members of the Court inclined toward nonpreferentialism—it is clear how powerful Story's work continues to be. In a better position than most to affect Supreme Court doctrine, Story ensured a decidedly Protestant position by the time the Court heard the Mormon cases. His vision of Protestant religiosity, rather than the idealism attributed to the Framers, would be the standard against which all religious minorities would struggle, and by which all free-exercise decisions would be measured.

A Change in the Weather

By the end of the nineteenth century, the United States would be a very different place from the one inhabited—and interpreted—by Justice Story. For the Court, the Civil War and the Fourteenth Amendment would change the relationship between the federal government and the states. But outside the courthouse, too, the very complexion of the nation would undergo significant change. Immigration (particularly, for our purposes, of those representing non-Protestant traditions) would begin to alter the nation's religious demographics, as would the continued growth of new religious traditions such as the Mormons, Jehovah's Witnesses, Seventh-Day Adventists, and others. Even Protestant Christianity would face great change, as the conflicts over fundamentalism and modernism would split denominations and shake the "confidence of culture" that had been a hallmark of the beginning of the century.

What historian Robert Handy identifies as the "second disestablishment" (1991)—the beginning of the end of Republican Protestantism in American public culture—was beginning to take shape. Protestant organizations, which had for most of the century enjoyed legal privileges as a result of their overwhelming numbers—not just in making the rules, but in having the rules shaped to their benefit—began to see others (either non-Protestants or Protestants of questionable theological status) enjoying the same legal benefits. A perfect example is the "Peace Policy" instituted under President Grant, which enlisted religious organizations to assist in pacifying Native Americans as the nation expanded westward. When the federal funds were directed to Protestant organizations, there was no problem, and the coincidence of (Protestant) Christianity and culture was preserved. But when it was realized that Catholics and Quakers were not only eligible for the same funds, but were among the largest recipients of the federal monies, there arose within the established Protestant community a movement to separate religion from the dealings of the federal government (see Handy 1991).

Two articles capture well this transition from an American culture completely unaware of its basically Protestant foundations to one more cognizant of non-Protestants (and even different types of Protestants). In his article, legal historian Stuart Banner investigates the claim that Christianity was part of the common law (1998). Although he is able to find no evidence of its having any legal impact in courts throughout the nineteenth century, he also notes (without comment, but of central importance to us here) that the notion that Christianity was part of the common law, common enough in decisions written before and just after the Civil War, begins to disappear entirely by the end of the nineteenth century—even in cases where judges felt the need to refute the claim, rather than to just offer it as truth. Political scientist Frank Way makes the point more directly in his article (powerfully titled "Death of the Christian Nation") tracing state decisions for cases that presume a Protestant worldview—such as blasphemy prosecutions, Sunday closing cases, church property cases, and Bible reading cases (1987). He notes that, though once common, by the end of the nineteenth century, these types of cases were either becoming less common or were (as in the case of church property disputes) developing legal reasoning that did not privilege Protestant (or more generally Christian) notions of orthodoxy.

Both articles point to the changes at work in the legal world by the end of the nineteenth century. The Protestant presumptions upon which Justice Story had built his notions of religious freedom were being dismantled; notions of conscience were becoming more diverse than those held by Calvinist Christianity, as were the religious options available to those consciences. Seeming somewhat prescient—and a bit uncharacteristic, given his conservative, traditionalist character—Story would write in 1825 that it was "obvious that the law must fashion itself to the wants, and in some sort to the spirit of the age" (Schwartz 1995: 102). In the next chapter, we see how.

Notes

1. Special thanks to Amber Scheu for her assistance in some of the research for this section.

2. Ironically, this passage was published at the same time the last remnants of an established state church were being dismantled in his native Massachusetts, though still amidst state religious restrictions over public participation.

4

E Unum Pluribus: Out of One, Many

Throughout the nineteenth century, Protestant conceptualizations determined how religion was understood in the law, even as the entire matter seemed subsumed under the question of federalism. However, as the question of federalism played itself out, so too did the dominance of Republican Protestantism, and the two constituent elements in the church-state relationship—church and state—would undergo significant transformation as a result. In the end, it would take a transformation outside the realm of religion at the beginning of the twentieth century to advance the notion of expanded rights of individual conscience beyond the Protestant foundation laid by Justice Story and his Supreme Court colleagues in the nineteenth century. But even that transformation would build upon the Protestant foundation already established.

The "Church" in Church-State

As we noted in the previous chapter, even though Justice Story had played such an instrumental role in the earliest formations of religious liberty jurisprudence, he was unable to predict changes in American society that would threaten the monopoly enjoyed by Republican Protestantism. Immigration of increasing numbers of non-Protestants, the emergence of sectarian religious communities (most notably the Mormons, Seventh-Day Adventists, Jehovah's

Witnesses, and Christian Scientists), and the contentious fracturing of American Protestantism into modernist and fundamentalist wings put the lie to the notion of one unified Protestant culture. After 1878 fewer and fewer mainstream Protestants were involved as litigants in Supreme Court cases addressing issues of religious liberty; cases increasingly arose over questions about how the law should respond to increasing religious diversity.

Nonetheless, even by the beginning of the twentieth century, there was little doubt that doctrines and definitions embedded within Protestant Christianity still wielded extraordinary power, particularly as they related to the law and how it treated those who were not part of the Protestant mainstream. As we noted, freedom of religion was defined in Calvinist terms—not a matter of personal choice, but a matter of (religious) self-understanding compelled by (religious) conscience. The free exercise of religion meant the freedom to believe and worship; other activities could be restricted—whether they were considered by the believer to be religiously motivated or not.

Just as significant, however, was the identification of "religion" with institutional religion and collective religious identity in areas related to religious liberty. Throughout the nineteenth century, the law permitted an individual little room to deviate from socially accepted norms of congregation- or denomination-based identity; all Jews were generally considered to be alike, all Native Americans were generally considered to be the same, and so on.[1] Part of the reason for this habit in American public culture was probably the low level of diversity extant in the young nation—there were simply fewer models of religious individuality then than there are today (with all due respect to the arguments of Butler 1990, Hatch 1989, and Moore 1986). It is also likely that the comparatively large role played by religion as a marker of identity (not only theological, but also cultural, historical, ethnic, and even political) throughout the eighteenth and nineteenth centuries (as compared to the last few decades of the twentieth century) encouraged people to think of others in stereotypical terms. Further explanation for this habit of thinking about religion in terms of institution-based collective identities might be found in the notion, common throughout the Western religious tradition, of the role of the community in the process of salvation. In Judaism and Christianity, the community—the "chosen people" or "Church"—had been the basic unit of religious meaning for centuries. Even the Protestant Reformation, founded on the notions of the priesthood of all believers and a personal relationship with the Divine, did not eliminate the role of the church; John Calvin himself had distinguished between the "visible" church ("the institution apparent to everyone in the world," which contains "both the elect and non-elect") and the "invisible" church ("the real church that contains only the elect") (Peterson 1993: 199). Given all of these cultural assumptions, it is not surprising that notions of individual rights and liberties with which we are familiar today were generally unheard of at the end of the nineteenth century, particularly as they related to religion. Rights—such as they were—were based on one's affiliations.

Examples of this collective and institutional understanding of religion abound in the nineteenth century. One of the best can be found in a body of litigation involving members of the Mormon community in Utah. The landmark *Reynolds* decision—which we discussed briefly in the previous chapter and which so clearly embodied Justice Story's Calvinist notions—did not directly prohibit George Reynolds from practicing plural marriage.[2] Rather, it affirmed Congress's authority to enact legislation that affected all Mormons, not only those who might engage in the act of polygamy, but also those who might support it or advocate it. More to the point, it affirmed Congress's right to enact legislation like the Morrill Act (1862), which made polygamy a crime in U.S. territories; the Edmunds Act (1882), which made polygamy a felony, disenfranchised polygamists, and made those who endorsed polygamy ineligible for jury service; and the Edmunds-Tucker Act (1887), which required an oath foreswearing belief in polygamy for eligibility to vote, serve on juries, and hold public office. These laws not only prohibited polygamy but also penalized the Church, so that, by the end of the 1880s, the entirety of Mormondom faced the dilemma of either capitulating on the two related issues of plural marriage and Church political control of the Utah Territory or being completely and forcibly liquidated by the federal government (see Mazur 1999).

Other examples of the Court's reliance on an institution-based definition of religious identity can be found in the decisions about conflicts over draft laws, conscientious objection, and naturalization.[3] In 1918, ruling in the *Selective Draft Law Cases*, the Supreme Court affirmed Congress's authority to exempt from service members of the clergy and seminary students and to provide alternative service for members of particular "peace" churches (such as the Amish, Mennonites, Brethren, and others), but made no provisions for religious traditions that had no established clergy or required no seminary training or those *individuals* who had a personal objection to warfare. (This would be the standard until 1965. Members of the Jehovah's Witnesses would litigate this issue throughout the 1940s and 1950s; taking John Calvin at his word, they argued that all members were priests and therefore eligible for clergy exemption from military service.)

Even in cases that didn't involve nonmajoritarian Protestants, we can find evidence of an institution-based, collective religious identity being applied by the Court. We mentioned in the previous chapter the large number of church property cases litigated throughout the nineteenth century. If we remove those cases involving conflicts over wills, donations, or taxes, we find that—in cases involving property disputes following the fragmentation of a congregation (or denomination)—the Supreme Court often used principles that seemed democratic but were in fact based on religious (and, given the makeup of the Court, primarily Protestant) notions of religious identity. At times, this meant trying to figure out which party in the dispute retained the highest number of original congregants; at other times it meant identifying the party that was the closest to the original teachings of the congregation (or denomination). While others have examined the ramifications of courts being in a position to determine religious orthodoxy (see Way 1987), we are much more interested in the pattern revealed by this nineteenth-century practice. It seems to be an example of the High Court (and lower courts) understanding religious identity not only as static but also as determined by the community, whether that community is numeric or historic. In other words, in many of these cases the Court was often involved in an effort to determine which party represented the "one true church" (see, for example, *Smith v. Swormstedt*, 1853; *Watson v. Jones*, 1871; *Bouldin v. Alexander*, 1872 and 1880).

Of course, in these cases—as well as those involving Mormons, conscientious objectors, and others—the Court's use of a general, collective concept of religious identity had as much to do with how the Court functioned as it did with any definition of religious identity. Whether it was with the Morrill Act during the Civil War or the Selective Draft Law during World War I, the Supreme Court was not ruling on the rights or privileges of George Reynolds to engage in plural marriage or Mr. Arver to avoid the draft—so uninterested was the Court in Arver's specific plight that his first name was never mentioned in the decision! Rather, the Court was ruling on the legality of the law in conflict before them. It was Congress that had written into law the kinds of generalizations that seemed to affirm institution-based, tradition-based, or stereotypical identities that were to come before the Court. But given the Court's history of Republican Protestantism and its subsequent attitude toward matters of religious belief and behavior, it seemed to be in no hurry to change how it functioned in this area. In the two landmark cases in which individuals had asked the Supreme Court to overrule as unconstitutional laws regarding religion, it had either denied jurisdiction (*Permoli*) or refused (*Reynolds*).

The Supreme Court thus entered the twentieth century much as it had the nineteenth, decidedly *not* thinking about religion. Not coincidentally, it was not thinking much about individual rights or liberties either. Constitutional historian Robert McCloskey affirms this point, noting that the Court had yet to seriously consider "the liberties of man as man and not primarily as an economic animal"—that is, one affected by questions of property and business issues that had been close to the Court's heart since Marshall and Story. And, he notes, there were historic and structural reasons for this; except during times of war, the police powers that regulated individual rights were matters for the states. "Given these facts," he concludes, "it is easy to see why civil rights cases had been a minor item on the Court's docket"

(McCloskey 1960: 170–71). Quite possibly because Protestantism had such a firm grasp on the formulation of the earliest judicial theories regarding religion and its relationship to government, it would take a revolution on the Court (in an area other than religion) to bring about a fuller understanding of the individual rights of conscience and finally bring it closer to that articulated by the Framers over one hundred years earlier.

The "State" in Church-State

In addition to the changes in religious demographics altering the American landscape by the end of the nineteenth century, we must examine another, parallel change taking place that would be just as significant to the disestablishment of Republican Protestantism and therefore to the rise of greater individual liberty as envisioned by the Framers. This parallel change consisted of the growing self-confidence of the federal government and the subsequent emergence of an independent (and many might argue, secular) national political culture distinct from (and at times at odds with) the once-dominant Protestant culture. This change would threaten the monolith of Republican Protestantism in the early decades of the twentieth century and lead the way for greater individual freedoms, as well as set the stage for debates over the authority of Protestant religion in public policy with which we are so familiar today.

The secular aspect of this transformation is nicely illustrated in one small, seemingly insignificant moment late in the nineteenth century. For the first one hundred years of the nation's history, interactions with Native American tribes had been conducted by treaty (made by the president, ratified by the Senate). However, in the early 1870s, the House of Representatives asserted control over the issue (in the form of a rider to an appropriations bill), with no apparent response from the Senate. While this might seem trivial, it symbolizes the growing self-confidence of the federal government, particularly when we keep in mind the context of Native American relations with the federal government. During the colonial period, Native Americans—taken as a collective identity, which, as we have noted, they often were by the federal government—represented one of the handful of political entities in competition for control of the continent, alongside the British, the French, and the Spanish (Bowden 1981). As long as the British were competing with the French and Spanish, the Native American were often seen as leverage or political allies. Inasmuch as they were players in an international competition, they were therefore handled by the Senate and the president. However, once the threat of alliances with the French and Spanish was removed (and North-South sectional distractions were reduced), the federal government could treat all Native Americans as an internal issue rather than an international threat, and thus the House assumed primary responsibility for their care. The nation was establishing itself from coast to coast, and Native Americans had lost their leverage.

In matters religious, we find another illustration at roughly the same historical moment. President Grant's "peace policy," which we mentioned briefly in the previous chapter—a policy that spent federal dollars in exchange for the pacification of Native Americans—was one that benefited many religious traditions, not just the established Protestant mainstream. And while we noted that this was the cause of some discomfort for some of those mainstream denominations who did not want Quakers and Catholics to benefit, the federal government—at least in terms of the money distributed—was virtually unconcerned with who got the money, as long as the military (rather than religious) goals were met. In other words, the federal government was not particularly interested in missionizing Native Americans, or in subsidizing only mainstream Protestant missionary organizations to do so; it was concerned with expanding the frontier west, and safeguarding the means to do so. If missionizing the Native Americans (by Protestants, Catholics, or whomever) would pacify them, so be it (see Handy 1991).

But the Protestant worldview that had so informed American civic development would not disappear from sight (many would argue that it lingers still—see Sarna 1990), and evidence of it abounds in the public record. In a classic statement bringing the two (now often competing) elements of Republican Protestantism and self-confident secular government together, Supreme Court Justice Sutherland noted in a 1931 naturalization case that

> We are a Christian people, according to one another the equal right of religious freedom, and acknowledging with reverence the duty of obedience to the will of god. But, also, we are a nation with a duty to survive; a nation whose Constitution contemplates war as well as peace; whose government must go forward upon the assumption, and safely can proceed upon no other, that unqualified allegiance to the nation and submission and obedience to the laws of the land, as well as those made for war as those made for peace, are not inconsistent with the will of God. (*United States v. Macintosh*, 1931)

The case, involving a Canadian who refused to agree to take up arms as a condition for becoming an American citizen, nicely illustrates the dilemma between Republican Protestantism, which had informed American public culture since its founding, and the needs and demands of an increasingly self-aware, increasingly powerful federal government. We are all Christians, Sutherland suggests in standard Republican Protestant terms, but we are also a nation, and the needs of the nation overrule the needs of the individual citizens of that nation.

Given the nature of this statement, it is not surprising that, in the first three decades of the twentieth century, as the federal government was becoming increasingly independent of its Republican Protestant roots, the type of conflict in which Macintosh found himself—between Christian morality and the demands of the nation-state—would make regular appearances before the Supreme Court. It is likely no coincidence that the conflicts with religion from the end of the Civil War to the beginning of World War II embody this conflict, with mainstream as well as nonmainstream Protestants involved. The Mormon conflict we discussed earlier involved, at least in part, a conflict between the Mormon leadership and Congress over the authority to control territory (Mazur 1999). The conflicts over military service involved many young men who, for religious reasons, refused to assist with the military demands of the government (see, for example, *Hamilton v. Regents of the University of Califor-*

nia, 1934). And although a number of conflicts over naturalization did not involve the pacifistic claims of a particular religious tradition (see *United States v. Schwimmer*, 1929), others did (*Macintosh* and *United States v. Bland*, 1931), and all pitted the claims of individual conscience against the needs of the nation-state. Sociologist Steve Bruce has recently argued that "the decline of religion permits the freedom of the individual" (2003: 244). If this is so, it was only made possible in the American legal system by putting some distance between the federal government and its Republican Protestant heritage.

Free Speech, Religion, and the "Revolution" of 1937

Because the Fourteenth Amendment serves as such an important symbolic benchmark in most discussions of the freedom of conscience, we can now return to the eighteenth century—with our understanding of the growing self-confidence of the federal government—to better understand this amendment's role in the development of individual rights of conscience. While today it is accepted constitutional doctrine (even among the nonpreferentialists on the Supreme Court) that the Fourteenth Amendment exerts federal control over the states—particularly in the area of individual rights—and thereby protects believers from state as well as federal misbehavior, the historical evidence suggests a different intention. McCloskey suggests that the *Slaughter-House* decision (1873) "rejected the contention that the privileges or immunities clause [of the Fourteenth Amendment] protected such rights" (1960: 170). Daniel Conkle notes that the debates in 1875–1876 over the Blaine Amendment (which was named for its sponsor, Rep. James Blaine [R–Maine] and which repeated nearly verbatim the two religion clauses of the First Amendment, while applying the prohibitions explicitly to the states) never centered on the repetition it seemed to represent. In other words, even though the Blaine Amendment was defeated, no one considered it superfluous or a repetition of the First Amendment because no one yet understood the Fourteenth Amendment as applying the First Amendment to the states (Conkle 2003: 22). Indeed, McCloskey concludes, "as late as 1922 the

Court denied that the [Fourteenth] Amendment restricted the states in dealing with freedom of expression," or, by implication, any of the other aspects of the First Amendment (1960: 170).

What the Fourteenth Amendment did do, however, was initiate a period in which the Supreme Court, no longer facing questions of federalism, became the guarantor of the rights of businessmen in their struggles against intrusive governmental regulation—a period of economic laissez-faire that would last into the third decade of the twentieth century. The fulcrum of this protection was found in the Due Process Clause, which was increasingly used by the Supreme Court to protect the right of businessmen to form agreements with their employees free of government restrictions—the "right of contract." However, this interpretation was instrumental in the development of cases involving individual liberties like freedom of conscience. It placed the federal courts in the center of disputes between the government and the individual and made them the guarantors of individual—rather than collective—rights. Concludes McCloskey: "In a way the development of the due process clause to protect economic rights made the ultimate protection of other rights logically inescapable" (1960: 171).

Beginning at the turn of the twentieth century, a variety of diverse and seemingly unrelated circumstances would have a profound effect on the direction of the Court. First, the addition of justices like Oliver Wendell Holmes Jr. (1902) and Louis Brandeis (1916) would bring strong libertarian voices to the Court. Second, the events leading up to and including World War I and the Russian Revolution would elicit from the increasingly self-confident federal government policies, such as the Espionage Act (1917) and the Sedition Act (1918), that placed limits on the rights of individual expression, necessitating Court involvement. "The American government," writes Claudia Isler, "became obsessed with silencing political opinion" (2001: 28), and as a result, an increasing number of challenges to these laws found their way to federal courts, and eventually to the Supreme Court.

It is through these cases, which often did not involve religion, that we begin to see an expansion of liberty rights and thus an expansion of individual rights of conscience. For example, in *Schenck v. United States* (1919), the Court ruled for the first time on a claim involving a congressional restriction of the First Amendment right to freedom of expression. While ruling that during ordinary times Schenck, a Socialist, might have prevailed in his case, his organization's leaflets urging men to resist the draft presented a "clear and present danger" during a time of war and could therefore be restricted (and those responsible for them punished). Six years later, the Supreme Court asserted federal authority over state actions with regard to individual rights of expression stipulated in the First Amendment. In *Gitlow v. New York* (1925), a case involving New York's criminal anarchy statute, Justice Sanford writing for the majority noted that "we may and do assume that freedom of speech and of the press—which are protected by the First Amendment from abridgment by Congress—are among the fundamental personal rights and 'liberties' protected by the due process clause of the Fourteenth Amendment from impairment by the States."[4]

This "assumption" of First Amendment application to state action was becoming part of federal jurisprudence. In his own concurrence in the *Hamilton* decision (mentioned earlier), Justice Cardozo extended the First Amendment's coverage even further. "I assume for present purposes," he wrote, "that the religious liberty protected by the First Amendment against invasion by the nation is protected by the Fourteenth Amendment against invasion by the states." In 1937, in a decision involving double jeopardy claims in a death penalty case, Justice Cardozo—writing for the majority this time—would finally expand the coverage of the Fourteenth Amendment to the entirety of the First Amendment (as well as the Sixth Amendment) when he wrote that

> the due process clause of the Fourteenth Amendment may make it unlawful for a state to abridge by its statutes the freedom of speech which the First Amendment safeguards against encroachment by Congress . . . or the like freedom of the press . . . or the free exercise of religion . . . or the right of peaceable assembly, without which speech would be unduly trammeled . . . or the right of one accused of a crime to the benefit of counsel. In these and other situations immunities that are valid as against the federal government by the force of specific pledges of particular amendments have been found to be implicit in the concept of ordered liberty, and thus, through the Fourteenth Amendment, become valid as against the states. (*Palko v. Connecticut*, 1937; internal citations removed)

Following the logic of Justice Stone's decision in *United States v. Carolene Products Company* (1938), McCloskey argues that "free expression (including of course religious expression) occupied a 'preferred position' in America's constellation of constitutional rights, and that government action impinging on it was presumptively invalid" (1960: 194).

It is worth noting that, even as the Court was expanding the authority of the Fourteenth Amendment to include more of the First Amendment, it was still primarily focused on economic policy. However, the reelection of Franklin Roosevelt in 1936, and the introduction of Roosevelt's plan to bypass the Court's rejection of numerous elements of the New Deal by expanding the number of justices (the so-called court-packing plan), signaled the end of the Court's preoccupation with economics in the same way the Civil War had signaled the end of the Court's preoccupation with issues of federalism. After one justice reversed position and several others retired and were replaced, the Court affirmed the federal government's role in establishing economic policy, and the so-called switch in time that saved nine became the beginning of a period of concentration on civil rights and liberties that would become the hallmark of the remainder of their twentieth-century work. "Since 1937," note constitutional scholars Henry Abraham and Barbara Perry, "the overwhelming majority of judicial vetoes imposed upon the several states and almost all of those against the national government have been invoked because they infringed personal liberties other than those of 'property,' safeguarded under the Constitution," up from 2 out of 160 decisions in the 1935–1936 term to 80 out of 149 in the 1979–1980 term (1998: 4–5).

Talking the Talk, Walking the Walk

By 1940, the Jehovah's Witnesses had brought a small handful of cases to the Supreme Court, mostly with mixed results. That year, in the case of *Minersville School District v. Gobitis* (which involved Jehovah's Witness children and their right to refuse to salute the flag in school), Witness president Joseph Rutherford (rather than legal counsel Olin Moyle) presented the oral arguments to the Supreme Court. Rutherford had himself briefly been imprisoned (along with a number of his staff) under the Espionage Act (1917) and was therefore no stranger to both the power of the federal government and the issues at stake in free speech litigation. However, his presentation relied on religious, almost theological arguments—he was described as being like a "pontifical religious leader" (Stevens 1973: 78)—rather than on free speech grounds, and the Supreme Court, under the authorship of Justice Frankfurter, found for the school district.

That same year, the Supreme Court would hear another case involving Jehovah's Witnesses, *Cantwell v. Connecticut* (about which we go into greater detail in the next chapter). What is most significant for our purposes here, however, is the difference in the manner in which these two cases were argued. *Cantwell* involved two Witnesses preaching in public and being charged with preaching without a license as well as breach of the peace. While religious justifications were clearly present, the Witness organization also relied in part on arguments stemming from free speech rights similar to those successfully litigated in the previous decades before the Court. And as we see in the next chapter, the Witnesses were triumphant.

It is interesting to note the relationship between religious liberty and free speech in these (and other) Jehovah's Witness cases and their efficacy with the Supreme Court. During a period of nearly thirty years of regular Supreme Court litigation, in those instances when the organization based its arguments on religious liberty justifications alone, the cases were either denied a hearing by the Court or resulted in decisions adverse to the organization. In those instances when the organization based its arguments either on a combination of free speech and religious liberty rights, or on free speech rights alone, the organization was much more likely to triumph (see Mazur 1999).

It makes perfect sense that free speech, rather than religious liberty as such, would be the entry point for expanded individual rights of conscience. Given the legacy of Republican Protestantism, it was unlikely that religious communities such as the Mormons or the Native Americans would persuade the Supreme

Court that religious behaviors seen either as deviant or heretical (or even as nonreligious) should be tolerated, much less granted rights of free exercise. Entirely Protestant until 1836 (when its first Catholic was seated) and entirely Christian until 1916 (when its first Jew was seated), the Court represented the nation well, and understood the world in largely Protestant terms. However, Jehovah's Witness theology was directly related to conservative Protestant theology, more so, it probably seemed, than Mormonism and Native American religious traditions. In addition, as the Jehovah's Witnesses were making no threats to the physical authority of the nation—they may not participate fully as citizens, but they did not make any exclusive claims on any real estate anywhere—their pleas for tolerance were no greater threat than pacifists, socialists, atheists, or others who refused to pick up arms or refused to refrain from protesting. And finally, it was becoming clearer that the argument articulated by Justice Cardozo in *Palko*— that freedom of thought and speech was "the matrix, the indispensable condition, of nearly every other form of freedom" (327)—expanded the freedom of speech to include religious speech. Jehovah's Witnesses were able to take advantage of this trend, and as a result the connection between freedom of thought and freedom of speech became inseparable from the freedom of conscience and—given the historical trend of connecting conscience with religion—religious liberty.

In 1944, in an article that appeared in the *Minnesota Law Review*, retired state judge Edward Waite would give the Witnesses full credit for the expansion of free speech rights. Even today, many of the decisions involving Jehovah's Witnesses are considered landmark in the area of free speech *rather than* in the area of religious liberty, even though that speech was motivated by religious conscience. After 1940, it would be increasingly difficult to separate issues of free speech from those of religious speech. And with the admission by the Court that an action (such as speaking) was as significant as a belief, the definition of an individual's freedom of conscience would continue to be profoundly expanded.

Notes

1. Congressional Republicans have continued this generalizing form of stereotyping, recently claiming that Democratic opposition to certain judicial nominees who oppose abortion was a form of anti-Catholicism. The anachronistic lunacy of this claim is made clear if one recognizes that individual Catholics (and members of all other religious communities as well) differ on matters of doctrine. At the beginning of the twentieth century, it was communal doctrine rather than individual conviction that most concerned the Court. For reasons explained by Wuthnow (1988) and developed here and in subsequent chapters, this emphasis on communal doctrine gave way to an emphasis on individual belief both in public culture and in legal decision making.

2. Although "plural marriage" and "polygamy" seem to be interchangeable terms, we use the first term specifically to identify the Mormon religious practice, while we use the second term to identify the crime as prohibited by the federal government. The act envisioned by both terms, of course, is identical, but the difference in how it is viewed was central in the dispute.

3. The American government would often use a similar form of collective identity when dealing with Native Americans; despite vast cultural diversity across Native American communities, they were generally considered by the federal government as if they were all alike. However, because of the way in which Native American relations evolved in the United States, religious liberty claims involving traditional Native American religion would not come before the Supreme Court until near the end of the twentieth century (see Mazur 1999).

4. Affirming one point we made in the previous chapter, we note here that Justice Sanford cites Justice Story in his discussion of rights.

5

Separation of Church and State Expands[1]

As we have seen, the U.S. Supreme Court had little to say about church-state matters prior to 1940. Until the first decision relying on the First Amendment in 1845, the Supreme Court heard relatively few cases involving constitutional issues, but instead, when it addressed religion at all, adjudicated matters of statutory construction (nonconstitutional legal matters such as property, wills and taxes, naturalization, conscription, etc.). From 1845 to 1940, when the First Amendment was interpreted to control state as well as federal action (eventually via the Fourteenth Amendment), the Court heard fewer than a dozen cases raising constitutional questions related to religion (and most of those came between World War I and World War II). For the next three decades (from 1940 to 1970), it averaged about a case a year. However, since Warren Burger became Chief Justice in 1969 until the present, the Court has averaged slightly more than two church-state cases per year.

Several reasons can be offered that help to explain the rise in religious controversies that came to be settled by the U.S. Supreme Court. One is the fact that, as we discussed in chapter 3, the United States began as a de facto Protestant nation despite what its Constitution declares. The nation took a long time to awaken to the constitutional violations that even today some people cannot recognize. Laws requiring stores to close on the "Sabbath" have pretty much faded away, as have laws against blasphemy. But some Americans still seek government endorsement of prayer in public schools, for example, not realizing that pupils are free now to pray if they wish, providing only that it not disrupt classroom order. It is not just prayer in the schools these people seek, however, but government endorsement of that prayer, something the Establishment Clause clearly prohibits.

A second reason is, of course, the increase in religious pluralism in America. American society was, so to speak, born pluralistic, even if that meant chiefly multiple kinds of Protestant religion. The nineteenth century, however, brought massive waves of non-Protestants to the United States. Catholics, Jews, and Greek Orthodox came in great numbers, to a point where exclusionary laws were passed. And when those laws were rescinded, migration from the East blossomed, leading to large numbers of Hindus, Buddhists, and Muslims present in the United States.

A third, and interrelated, reason for increased religious controversies leading to court action is the growth of bureaucracy and hence of government regulations of behavior, including religious behavior. From building codes to government grants, from civil rights commissions to regulation of the airwaves, government at all levels has increasing occasion to intervene in public life, including religious public life. Absolute separation of church and state is impossible, therefore; for example, church buildings must conform to building codes, and clergy can marry only couples who have a government license to marry.

For these reasons (and probably others) the United States has expanded its interpretation of what "separation" of church and state means. Generally, this expansion has meant a wider understanding of: (1) what can be "freely exercised" as religion and (2) what is seen as an unconstitutional "establishment" of religion. This broader understanding of the religion clauses—what Mark DeWolfe Howe called "converting the liberal principle of tolerance into the radical principle of liberty" (1950: 172)—was not obvious at the beginning with the writing of the U.S. Constitution. (Although, as we saw in our opening chapters, it can be argued that at least Madison and Jefferson had a conception of church-state relations pretty close to the contemporary conception.) Instead, this contemporary conception dates from the *Cantwell* decision in 1940, a decision that set in motion big strides toward greater separation of church and state.

Toward Greater Separation

The U.S. Constitution requires of the Supreme Court only that it decide cases, not that it render reasons for its decisions. Given the importance of precedent in Anglo-American law, however, it is clear why, from the beginning, the Court has provided often elaborate justifications for its decisions. Not only are these justifications meant to explain to the losing side why it lost; in addition, everyone else is instructed about what will and will not be legal in similar cases.

The Supreme Court, however, deals only with cases that work their way to it. It has discretion as to the cases it will hear, and therefore it can wait until a case comes along that exhibits a constitutional issue the Court wants to clarify, but it cannot reach out to decide just any issue. This limitation on the Supreme Court is important here because it means that, until the adoption of the Fourteenth Amendment after the Civil War, which bit by bit extended federal constitutional rights into every state, the Supreme Court had cases coming largely from U.S. territories, which were not yet states. Its religion cases were few and far between.

Religiously Motivated Action

One notable exception was *Reynolds v. United States* (1878). Reynolds was a Mormon living in Utah territory with two wives. The U.S. Congress, which had jurisdiction over Utah, had passed a law making plural marriages in U.S. territories illegal, and Reynolds challenged that law. He lost, but what makes the case noteworthy is the fact that for the first time the Supreme Court employed the so-called belief-action distinction. The distinction was common enough even in colonial times, but now it became constitutional doctrine. The idea is simple: the Free Exercise Clause gives absolute freedom to *believe* as one chooses, but *actions* reflecting those beliefs are subject to government restraint. "Congress was deprived of all legislative power over mere opinion," wrote Chief Justice Waite, "but was left free to reach actions which were in violation of social duties or subversive of good order." The Court claimed that polygamy was indeed destructive of good order and therefore upheld the law in the face of Reynolds's challenge.

The belief-action distinction operated pretty much unchanged until 1940. Laws could be passed regulating behavior, and, as long as *religious* behavior was not specifically targeted, courts found such laws constitutional. In 1940, however, in *Cantwell v. Connecticut*, the Supreme Court reversed the conviction of a Jehovah's Witness who failed to seek a license in advance of playing in public a religious message on a portable phonograph. It was, in fact, a strongly anti–Roman Catholic message in a predominantly Roman Catholic neighborhood. Until 1940, courts would have rendered a guilty verdict—as the lower court did in this case—noting simply that it was a secular regulation being violated, a regulation that did not target Jehovah's Witnesses, or any religious group, but was applicable to all citizens.

In *Cantwell* the Supreme Court reversed the lower court's verdict, acknowledging that *religiously* motivated behavior can be constitutionally protected even though the same behavior, otherwise motivated, is not. It is important to note here that not only was the belief-action distinction being amended, but also— since obviously *some* religiously motivated actions are impermissible (for example, human sacrifice at the sacred altar) even as others are allowable—the Court had now to find some way to balance the interest on both sides of disputed actions.

In *Cantwell* the Court used the "clear and present danger" test used in free speech cases, finding that Cantwell represented no such danger. Over the next quarter century, however, a different test emerged, becoming regularized as the so-called Sherbert test, because it was made explicit in a 1963 case, *Sherbert v. Verner*. In that case Ms. Sherbert, a Seventh-Day Adventist, was fired because she refused to work on Saturday. The Court found that denying her unemployment compensation was an unconstitutional limitation on her free exercise of religion, a limitation, moreover, for which the state had no compelling justification.

As might be imagined, and can be seen clearly in retrospect, between *Cantwell* in 1940 and *Sherbert* in 1963 the Supreme Court was struggling with other free-exercise cases in which it faced the difficult question of *which* religious actions are entitled to special protection. As Justice Douglas wrote in one of these cases, "the rights with which we are dealing are not absolutes." Not by accident, many of the cases were brought by Cantwell's fellow Jehovah's Witnesses. To sell their religious literature could Witnesses be obliged to pay the tax that other "salesmen" paid? In 1942 the decision was *Yes*, by a vote of 5–4 (*Jones v. Opelika*). The following year, also on a 5–4 vote, that *Yes* vote was changed to *No* (*Murdock v. Pennsylvania*).

Very similar, in formal if not substantive terms, was the question of whether requiring Jehovah's Witness students to salute the flag violated their free exercise of religion, inasmuch as Witnesses regard flag saluting as idolatrous. In 1940, on a vote of 8–1, the Court said *No*, the state was justified in mandating the flag salute (*Minersville School District v. Gobitis*). However, the *Gobitis* decision was quickly recognized to be bad law; it was abandoned by the Court only three years later in a nearly identical case in which the Court ruled that the Witnesses' rights were violated by compelling the flag salute (*West Virginia State Board of Education v. Barnette*). (However, as we see in chapter 7, some on the current Court have attempted to revive *Gobitis* as the correct precedent in such cases.)

Close reading of those four cases, including dissents as well as majority opinions, establishes very clearly that the justices, in deciding when a religious action is subject to the same regulation that governs other actions, considered such questions as whether the regulation burdened the plaintiff's religious freedom and, if so, how great was this burden. They asked how important to the state was it to apply the regulation in every instance, and what would be the consequences of not doing so. And they inquired into possible alternative means the state might take to achieve a regulation's purpose without burdening the plaintiff's religious freedom. Thus, for example, in *Braunfeld v. Brown* (1961), certain Orthodox Jewish merchants claimed that the law requiring them to close down on Sundays impaired their free exercise of religion because, to remain commercially competitive, they would have to violate Orthodox law and work on Saturdays. Among the options the Court considered (and rejected) was an "alternative means" whereby the state would exempt from the Sunday closing law any person who, because of religious conviction, observed a day of rest other than Sunday.

As was stated earlier, the outcome of the deliberations in these (and other) free-exercise cases after 1940 led to the "Sherbert test," so-called because the majority opinion in *Sherbert v. Verner* is so clearly organized around certain questions that must be asked about the controversy. Justice Brennan, after introducing the facts in the case, wrote, "We turn first to the question whether the disqualification for benefits imposes any burden on the free exercise of appellant's religion" and responded that it does. He goes on, "We must next consider whether some compelling state interest . . . justifies the substantial infringement of appellant's First Amendment right" and finds none. Only if Sherbert's denial of unemployment compensation had been upheld by the Court would Brennan have gone on to ask the third question raised in *Braunfeld v. Brown*: Might the state have an alternative means of achieving its purpose without burdening Sherbert? In other cases since 1963 this third question has been added to the "burden" and "compelling interest" questions, and together they constitute the Sherbert test.

It is obvious that the mere existence of this test does not automatically render decisions, but it has lent system and continuity to subsequent cases. Generated by the *Cantwell* decision in 1940, which made ineffective the long-standing belief-action distinction and required the courts to find a basis for declaring some religiously motivated actions protected by the Free Exercise Clause while others are not, the Sherbert test has more or less become that basis. While alternative tests might be imagined, it is important to the argument here to realize that, having abandoned the belief-action distinction, the Supreme Court had no choice other than to devise *some* method for balancing the right of individuals to freely exercise their religion against the interests of the state in regulating certain kinds of behavior.

Applying the Sherbert Test

The Supreme Court has had numerous occasions since 1963 to apply the balancing strategy known as the Sherbert test. One dramatic instance—dramatic because the outcome was probably unexpected and was certainly provocative—was *Wisconsin v. Yoder* (1972). In this case, Amish parents won the right, contrary to Wisconsin law, to take their children out of public school after the eighth grade, arguing that any education past that point is no longer practical but instead "worldly" and thus evil in Amish theology. Just two decades earlier, the Court, in its decision desegregating the public schools of Topeka, Kansas, had declared education one of government's most important functions. Now, in 1972, the Court sided with the Amish parents, in effect saying that the burden imposed on them by Wisconsin's compulsory school attendance until age sixteen was greater than the less-than-compelling state's interest in keeping Amish children in school an additional two years. The balancing act was obvious.

It was also obvious in a 1977 case where the religious interest lost out, though this case was decided on statutory, not constitutional, grounds. In *Trans World Airlines, Inc. v. Hardison*, an employee of the airline, whose job took place in a maintenance base that operated around the clock every day, sued for his right to take Saturdays off. As a member of the Worldwide Church of God, Hardison was a Sabbatarian. The Court ruled against him on the grounds that his job was essential, and on weekends he was the only available person on his shift who could perform it. In effect, this case found (1) Hardison's free exercise was indeed burdened, but (2) TWA had a compelling interest in keeping its operation fully staffed, and (3) no alternative method, such as paying premium wages to a substitute to work an extra day, was available.

Other cases in which the religious interest lost out could be cited, though there is no need to go into detail. For example, an Orthodox Jewish psychiatrist in the Air Force was required to remove his yarmulke while in uniform indoors; the need for esprit de corps and discipline was cited as compelling. Muslim prisoners who worked as trusties outside the prison walls were not granted the special privilege of returning to prison for noon prayers on the grounds that two sets of guards would be needed if the gang was split up, and gang morale would be jeopardized by unequal amounts of labor required of Muslim and non-Muslim. A Native American father was told that the state had a legitimate compelling interest in requiring his daughter to have a Social Security Number to qualify for federal government aid programs, even though the father believed that assigning his daughter a number robbed her of her soul.

It is enough for the purposes of this chapter simply to note that a balancing act, with *Sherbert* as the model, was the way by which these cases—and others that could be cited—were decided. Irrespective of which side won, questions of burden, compelling interest, and possible alternatives by which free exercise might be less burdened were addressed and weighed. As Ronald B. Flowers, long an observer of church-state court cases, says (1994: 44):

> Since 1963 the Court's view of the scope of the Free Exercise Clause, and consequently the amount of religious freedom available to the American people, has varied. For most of the period, when the "Sherbert test" was the principle for interpreting the clause, Americans enjoyed a large amount of freedom for religious practice. Those in specialized environments like the military did not enjoy the full range of this freedom, but decisions in these areas had little implication for the general population.

What Is Religious?

The Court had, in *Cantwell* and similar cases, created another troubling question that it could not dodge: What *is* religious? If, in abandoning the belief-action distinction, the law would protect some actions only if they were religiously motivated, the law needed some way to identify what is religious. It is perhaps no coincidence that during the quarter century the Court was evolving the Sherbert test it was wrestling with this second question too. Its resolution, while conceptually clear, is, like the Sherbert test, not easily applied.

The evolution of the answer to this second question began in 1944 in *United States v. Ballard*. Guy Ballard and his family led the I AM movement, which, among other things, made claims of being able to cure diseases that doctors called incurable. These claims were made in mailings to people, asking for the payment of money in exchange for the spiritual cure. Because the U.S. Post Office was involved, the government brought suit against the Ballards, charging fraud. In effect, then, the government was saying that the I AM movement's doctrines were not true and that the Ballards knew they were not true. The trial judge, however, instructed the jury that they were to decide not whether the doctrines were true but only whether the Ballards *believed* them to be true. On that basis the defendants were acquitted, and the government appealed to the Supreme Court.

The *Ballard* case is vitally important for the story here because it argued the point that government must not get involved in determining the truth or falsity of any religion—indeed, must not even define religion. Justice Douglas, for the majority, wrote:

> Heresy trials are foreign to our Constitution. Men may believe what they cannot prove. . . . The religious views espoused by respondents might seem incredible, if not preposterous, to most people. But if those doctrines are subject to trial before a jury charged with finding their truth or falsity, then the same can be done with the religious beliefs of any sect.

As stark as the majority opinion was, Justice Jackson would have gone even further. Deciding what is or is not religion, Jackson wrote in dissent, "is precisely the thing the Constitution put beyond the reach of the prosecutor, for the price of freedom of religion or of speech or of the press is that we must put up with, and even pay for, a good deal of rubbish."

This position of the Court's neutrality with respect to the definition of religion was foreshadowed in the nineteenth-century "church property" disputes. In those cases, the judges came to see that they were behaving as an ecclesiastical court whenever they took on the task of deciding which faction in an ownership quarrel was more faithful to the church's "original" doctrine and polity. Just as the courts then decided they were exceeding their constitutional authority, so did the Court in *Ballard* conclude that it must not decide the "truth" of any religion because this would, in effect, be deciding what is and is not religion.

An uncritical reading of *United States v. Ballard* might lead to the supposition that government really must maintain a hands-off policy when it comes to defining religion. Alas, as we shall now see, that has proved to be impossible.

From Religion to Conscience

Just as the *Cantwell* decision—which found that action motivated by religion is protected but the same action otherwise motivated is not—forced onto the Court the task of identifying religious motivation, so did the *Ballard* case force onto the Court the task of determining the subject matter of the Religion Clauses. And just as the *Sherbert v. Verner* case was the symbolic accomplishment of the first task, so was the task launched by *Ballard* accomplished with a clear-cut case in 1965 (*United States v. Seeger*), in which a self-proclaimed nonreligious person was unanimously granted the status of conscientious objector to war. As with the evolution of *Cantwell* to *Sherbert*, so too with the evolution of *Ballard* to *Seeger*: A series of decisions between *Ballard* and *Seeger* can, in retrospect, be seen to have made the outcome all but inevitable.

Soon after *Ballard* the Supreme Court was asked to rule on the constitutionality of parochial school students' use of tax revenue funds to get to school by public bus (*Everson v. Board of Education*, 1947). In finding this subsidy permissible, the Court went on to say that "neither a State nor the Federal Government can constitutionally force a person to profess a belief or disbelief in any religion." The message of *Ballard*—that government may not judge the truth or falsity of any religion—was once again affirmed.

It was also affirmed when the judicial system was asked whether humanistic or nontheistic "religious" organizations were entitled to tax exemption. Members of such groups looked upon them as the equivalent of churches, often meeting on Sundays to sing hymns, hear sermons, and take up collections of money. Were they not also eligible for tax exemption? In 1957, in *Fellowship of Humanity v. County of Alameda*, an appellate court ruled that such groups are entitled to the same tax exemption given to ordinary churches. To deny them that privilege, the California court said, would be to favor theism over nontheism, something clearly prohibited because it required a judgment about the *content* of belief. Instead, stated the court, the judgment should be based on the belief's *function*—"whether or not

the belief occupies the same place in the lives of its holders that
. . . orthodox beliefs occupy in the lives of believing majorities."

In 1961, the Supreme Court faced another kind of issue in which the state's authority to impose religious (or irreligious) belief was questioned. A year earlier, the Maryland Court of Appeals, the highest court in that state, had upheld the denial of a notary public commission for Roy R. Torcaso (*Torcaso v. Watkins,* 1960) because he refused to declare a belief in God as required by Maryland's constitution for positions of "profit or trust." Among other justifications for its decision, the court noted that

> to the members of the [Maryland Constitutional] Convention, as to the voters who adopted our [State] Constitution, belief in God was equated with a belief in moral accountability and the sanctity of an oath. We may assume that there may be permissible differences in the individual's conception of God. But it seems clear that under our [State] Constitution disbelief in a Supreme Being, and the denial of any moral accountability for conduct, not only renders a person incompetent to hold public office, but to give testimony, or serve as a juror. The historical record makes it clear that religious toleration, in which the State has taken pride, was never thought to encompass the ungodly.

This decision was overturned by the U.S. Supreme Court the following year in *Torcaso v. Watkins* (1961). The Court was following the logic declared in *Ballard, Everson,* and other cases that, in the ringing words of Justice Jackson, "The very purpose of the Bill of Rights was to withdraw certain subjects from the vicissitudes of political controversy."

In each of these cases we see the Supreme (or other) Court concluding that what once was *not* entitled to special treatment now *is,* which is to say that what *constitutes* religion has undergone considerable expansion. Nothing illustrates this expansion better than the 1965 *Seeger* case, and, five years later, *Welsh v. United States,* a case nearly identical to *Seeger.*

Conscientious objection has long been recognized in American law. At one point, membership in a so-called peace church (often Mennonite or Quaker) determined one's eligibility for that status, but over the years eligibility rules loosened some-what in recognition of the great variety of religious beliefs found in the United States. In 1948, Congress amended the Selective Service Act again, declaring that, for the purposes of draft boards, eligibility would be determined by one's

> religious training and belief [which] means an individual's be-lief in a relation to a Supreme Being involving duties superior to those arising from any human relation, but does not include essentially political, sociological, or philosophical views or a merely personal moral code. (50 United States Code App. ¶456 [j] 1958 ed.)

In the 1965 case, Seeger contended that, though he did not believe in a Supreme Being, he did have a "faith in a purely eth-ical creed" and thus was entitled to conscientious objector status. The Supreme Court agreed. His creed, the justices said, was the equivalent of a religion, which they characterized in the phrase a "sincere and meaningful belief which occupies in the life of its possessor a place parallel to that fulfilled by the God of those ad-mittedly qualifying for the exemption," virtually the same word-ing found in *Fellowship of Humanity v. County of Alameda*. Five years later, in *Welsh*, the majority opinion went even further in declaring eligible for exemption from military service "all those whose consciences, spurred by deeply held moral, ethical, or re-ligious beliefs, would give no rest or peace if they allowed them-selves to become a part of an instrument of war." The Court, as one legal scholar put it some years later, left "no room for any residual doubt." It "viewed deeply and sincerely held moral or ethical beliefs as the functional, and thus the legal, equivalent of religious beliefs. The justices had obfuscated any distinction be-tween religion and all other belief systems" (Ingber 1989: 260).

Three justices dissented in *Welsh*, suggesting something less than unanimity on exactly how conscientious objection cases are to be decided. But if the argument here is correct, even if *Seeger* and *Welsh* did not establish the principle that "conscience" is now the legal equivalent of "religion," those cases provide a rea-sonable basis for assuming that it is only a matter of time before it will be. Richards (1986: 131) states the case well:

Such cases suggest the guarantee of religious free exercise might encompass freedom of conscience as such. While the Supreme Court has drawn back from embracing any such clear statement of principle, the gravitational pull to this principle in the case of law is obvious, and it may be the most just interpretation of underlying constitutional principles.

As early as 1919, Harlan Fiske Stone, later justice (and then chief justice) of the Supreme Court, wrote (1919: 263), "While conscience is commonly associated with religious convictions, all experience teaches us that the supreme moral imperative which sometimes actuates men to choose one course of action in preference to another and to adhere to it at all costs may be dissociated from what is commonly recognized as religious experience."

In 1943, in *United States v. Kauten*, a Federal District Court exempted an atheist from the draft on the following grounds:

A conscience which categorically requires the believer to disregard elementary self-interest and to accept martyrdom in preference to transgressing its tenets . . . may justly be regarded as a response of the individual to an inward mentor, call it conscience or God, that is for many persons at the present time the equivalent of what has always been thought a religious impulse.

Given this unfolding of interpretations, how could conscience *not* eventually be recognized as the equivalent of religion? Such recognition came about not from mere changes in court personnel or mere volition on the part of those personnel. Rather, it resulted from pressures that mounted in America's history and social structure. At least two of these were massively influential: (1) increased religious pluralism and (2) increased government regulation—and thus intrusion—in citizens' lives, including their religious lives. When the First Amendment was drafted, religious freedom meant absolute freedom of belief, but religious behavior could be regulated as long as the Establishment Clause was not violated through differential treatment of religions. However, religious freedom came to be seen as honoring religiously motivated behavior, which meant that identifying what was truly religious became necessary. And *that* was seen as casting judges as "theologians," clearly an unconstitutional role.

For these reasons, the point was reached in judicial opera-
tions where questions of what and how religion was practiced
no longer mattered; instead, questions about sincerity and fervor
were asked. In other words, it was the *fact* of conviction, not the
content of that conviction, that the First Amendment was understood to protect. Free exercise now referred to *conscience*,
whether articulated in religious language or not.[2]

The Loss That Comes with Gain

Milton R. Konvitz makes this argument—that the Constitution protects conscience—in very strong terms. He speculates
(1968: 99) on how church-state history would be different had
the Framers worded the Religion Clauses to protect the "free exercise of conscience":

> This enlargement would have saved us much trouble. We
> would not have needed to worry over whether Ethical Culture
> or humanism is a religion, or whether the pacifism of a Seeger
> . . . is based on a religious belief. For at the heart of the beliefs
> of such men and movements is conscience, and persons who
> avow religious beliefs . . . do not hold a monopoly on con-
> science.

This last thought is profound indeed: If religious beliefs are
anchored in conscience, it is conscience that is primary and religion its possible derivative. In this perspective, religion is a *language* of conscience, but persons need not use a particular
language in order to make claims of conscience. As Konvitz per-
ceives, before *Seeger* and *Welsh* the Supreme Court had, in effect,
insisted that conscience "must speak as religion if it is to be
heard in the legal forum" (1968: 104). Or, as Justice Harlan wrote
in a concurring opinion in *Welsh*, "The constitutional question . . .
is whether a statute that defers to the individual's conscience
only when his views emanate from adherence to theistic religious beliefs is within the power of Congress."

Ironically, reservations about this development are expressed
from an unexpected quarter: historic peace churches. Although
the size of this objection is unknown, it will, in the long run, be
ineffective. Nonetheless, analysis of the objection does offer an

opportunity to explore a far more pervasive consequence of the constitutional recognition of the rights of conscience.

Moskos and Chambers describe a 1989 interdenominational and international conference on conscientious objection at which the keynote speaker, a member of a peace church (Church of the Brethren), complained that the World Council of Churches, in its policy statement regarding the conscientious objector, or CO, seemed to "legitimate conscientious objection more from a secular human rights perspective than from the Judeo-Christian imperative." The CO status, he went on, was "reduced to an individual state of distress and the foundation of the New Testament was disregarded" (quoted in Moskos and Chambers 1993: 200).

Now it might seem odd that a member of a church, one of whose central tenets is pacifism, would object to enlarging the numbers of persons entitled to have their pacifism recognized. From another perspective, however, a peace church loses something as nonmembers of peace churches win: the privilege, even the quasi-"establishment" status, it once had in society's interpretation of religious liberty. That loss can obviously be painful if only the loss, and not the gain, is perceived.

Consider the similar complaint of Richard John Neuhaus in his book *The Naked Public Square* (1984: 80):

> As time went on . . . the court's references to religion had less and less to do with what is usually meant by religion. That is, religion no longer referred to those communal traditions of ultimate beliefs and practice ordinarily called religion. Religion, in the court's meaning, became radically individualized and privatized. Religion became a synonym for conscience. . . . Thus religion is no longer a matter of content but of sincerity. It is no longer a matter of communal values but of individual conviction. In short, it is no longer a public reality and therefore cannot interfere with public business.

Stephen Carter (1993: 25) is likewise confounded:

> The message of contemporary culture seems to be that it is perfectly all right to believe that stuff—we have freedom of conscience, folks can believe what they like—but you really ought to keep it to yourself, especially if your beliefs are the sort that cause you to act in ways that are . . . well . . . a bit unorthodox.

One wonders if Carter could read those words aloud to Seeger or Welsh. Would he really sacrifice their rights of conscience in order to restore a privileged voice for "religion"?

What many have come to understand, as Neuhaus and Carter apparently have not, is that recognizing the rights of conscience *requires* a level verbal playing field. Conscientious claims, whether stated in religious or other terms, are equal, and adjudicating among those claims *requires* a language all can use meaningfully. Thus, what Neuhaus sees as a "naked public square"—the exclusion of religion from the conduct of public business—means merely the devaluation of religious authority in public political deliberation (Neuhaus 1984: vii). It by no means excludes conscience whether religiously conceived or not.

Ralph Lerner (1989: 88–89) understands how something is lost even as something is gained:

> [A]s far as federal constitutional law was concerned, the focus of attention was to be shifted from groups to individuals, from sects to consciences. The new enlightened regime . . . made a new world safe, not for church or chapel or synagogue, but for each and every believer, indeed for each and every person's private conscience. . . . American society under the Constitution was open to all kinds of voluntary associations, and . . . religionists who meant to enjoy the benefit of that regime had to quietly accept their place as one kind of association among many. Those unable to bear this muting of their clarion call would soon discover that society was equally uncomfortable with them. . . . Eschewing any pretensions to holiness or divine direction, this system of secular, enlightened indifference is large enough and generous enough to shield almost any kind of holiness so long as it minds its civil manners.

It is in minding its "civil manners," so to speak, that religion only appears to fade from view in the public square. It remains a voice in public deliberation but is no longer a *privileged* voice.

Strategic Events on the Path of Disestablishment

So far in this chapter, we have maintained (1) that what the Free Exercise Clause protects is increasingly understood to refer not just to religion in the traditional sense but to conscience and (2) that this enlarged understanding of free exercise was compelled once the courts rejected the belief-action distinction, thus requiring the law to differentiate actions that are secularly motivated from actions reflecting true conviction, whether articulated in religious language or not. Once it is recognized, however, that it is "conscience" that is protected—and not just "religion"—a rather startling implication becomes apparent: If conscience is what can be freely exercised, is it therefore also conscience that Congress must not establish? If so, just what does that mean? We explore these questions now.

Nonpreferentialism Exposed

It seems reasonable to expect that the greatest support for the free exercise of religion would come from persons who assign the greatest importance to religion. In one sense that is true, as exemplified in the very broad range of religious leaders included in the support given to the Reverend Sun Myung Moon in his tax evasion case. Carlton Sherwood has listed them (1991: 377–78):

> A stranger group of bedfellows would be hard to imagine: the Reverend Jerry Falwell, former Senator Eugene McCarthy, the late Clare Booth Luce, Harvard law professor Laurence Tribe, and Senator Orrin Hatch. . . . [A] single thread also ties together the liberal American Civil Liberties Union and the Southern Christian Leadership Conference with the conservative Freemen Institute. The same thread connects Baptists and Presbyterians, the Roman Catholic Church and the National Council of Churches, not to mention the avowedly Marxist Spartacist League as well as the states of Hawaii, Oregon, and Rhode Island. Between 1982 and 1984 all of the above and more than thirty other individuals and organizations entered *amicus curiae* . . . briefs [on Moon's behalf].

Moon lost his case despite the outpouring of support, but the reason for the concern is simple to understand. All the sponsors of those briefs could see that if the Internal Revenue Service could punish the founder and leader of the Unification Church on the grounds charged, it could similarly punish them; in the case of religious leaders, it was their own free exercise of religion that was in jeopardy. In any avowedly pluralistic society, then, each religion is likely to recognize that *its* welfare depends upon upholding the free exercise of *all* religions.

We saw earlier in this chapter, however, that at least some people of religious conviction decry the circumstances whereby "conscience" becomes entitled to the constitutional protection heretofore extended only to "religion." For Richard John Neuhaus, this means that courts look not at the content of belief but at the sincerity with which belief is held. "Individual conviction," he says, has replaced "communal values" (1984: 80).

We disagree. When individual conviction or conscience is regarded as religion's legal equivalent, religion as a "communal value" does not disappear, as Neuhaus seems to suggest. Rather, upon close inspection it turns out that communal religion (the "church" or other organized religious activity) merely has to share a governmental preference it alone once enjoyed, a preference now recognized to be unconstitutional. The more sensitive the state becomes in protecting conscience, in other words, the more likely it is to uncover heretofore unacknowledged "established" religion, which is then found to be in violation of the Establishment Clause. People who regret this jurisprudential development are often called "nonpreferentialists" because, while they agree that government cannot prefer one religion over another, they do believe government can and should prefer religion over irreligion.

The issue is clearly exhibited in the *Torcaso* case discussed earlier. The Supreme Court in that case, using language it had used before, ruled that government may not force a person "to profess a belief or disbelief in any religion" and thus declared unconstitutional Maryland's constitutional provision requiring a belief in God by anyone serving any public office. On the grounds, then, that Torcaso was free to disbelieve in God and still be a commissioned notary public, the state was compelled to "disestablish" a religious criterion (theistic belief) for taking office. Thus, following his lament that, when conscience became a synonym for religion, "communal values" were replaced by "individual conviction," Neuhaus goes on to say that religion "is no longer a public reality and therefore cannot interfere with public business" (1984: 80). This fact Neuhaus laments, but he misperceives the meaning of *Torcaso*: It is not that religion is no longer a public reality but rather that public reality includes a broader conception of religion.

It is not surprising that, when free exercise doctrine extends far enough to recognize consciences not articulated religiously, some people are vexed—not so much because conscientious persons receive benefits as because traditional forms of religion lose privileged status. This, of course, is not the wording used by those who are vexed. They would say, rather, that government is no longer accommodating traditional forms of religion. It is renewed accommodation of *their* religion that they desire, not the newly discovered accommodation of heretofore unprotected consciences. Marvin Frankel makes this point with hyperbole. Labeling as "access seekers" persons who want the wall of separation returned to a lower height, Frankel claims that "the concrete goals of the access seekers reflect mainly crabbed demands for status, authority, and petty but maddening superordination" (1992: 639).

Frankel's criticism may be harsh, but it does point up the inherent tension between the Free Exercise Clause and its Establishment counterpart, or—as some have put it—between the accommodation of religion that the Free Exercise Clause *requires* and the accommodation of religion that the Establishment Clause *permits*. Persons who support an interpretation of free exercise broad enough to extend to "conscience" seem likely to support an interpretation of establishment that finds unconstitutional many religious actions that have previously been accommodated. Put another way, when the rights of free exercise are extended to conscience or conviction, whether articulated religiously or not, heretofore religious actions that have been shown preference because they are *religious* are vulnerable to the charge that they represent an unconstitutional establishment of religion. The conscientious objection cases illustrate this point exactly: If conviction alone, and not identification with a *particular* kind of religious belief, is sufficient to claim conscientious objector status, it means that persons holding those particular beliefs were earlier enjoying an unconstitutional privilege.

Freedom of Conscience and the Establishment Clause

The inherent tension between the two clauses is illustrated in an unusually vivid way in a 1989 Supreme Court case, *County of Allegheny et al. v. American Civil Liberties Union et al.* At issue was the constitutionality of (1) a crèche scene installed in the lobby of Pittsburgh's City-County Building and (2) a Hanukkah menorah placed just outside a nearby building, next to a Christmas tree and a sign saluting liberty. The Court, with four dissenting votes, ruled to outlaw the crèche scene as clearly sending a message of governmental "endorsement" of an obviously Christian symbol, but it ruled in favor of the menorah on the grounds that the menorah, like the Christmas tree, has secular as well as religious connotations and thus could be interpreted as merely a symbol of the winter holiday season.

Ostensibly, these decisions were based on differing interpretations of the Establishment Clause, but the majority opinion—written by Justice Blackmun—and the dissenting opinion—written by Justice Kennedy—make clear that free-exercise considerations lay just beneath the surface of the debate. Our point here is that, because of the inherent tension between the two clauses, establishment-based decisions are likely to involve free-exercise issues as well. The so-called nonpreferentialists—those seeking greater accommodation for religion, but only religion traditionally conceived—do not appreciate this inherent relationship, as we shall now see.

Because the justices arrive at their opinions after circulating drafts of one another's tentative views of a case, it is not uncommon, in cases having dissenting minorities, for the final majority and minority opinions to include counterarguments as well as arguments. The Allegheny crèche case provides us with an especially vigorous, not to say vituperative, illustration.

After Blackmun introduces the facts of the crèche and the menorah, he first develops the line of reasoning he and other members of the majority have employed in arriving at their opinion.

> This Nation is heir to a history and tradition of religious diversity that dates from the settlement of the North American continent. Sectarian differences among various Christian denominations were central to the origins of our Republic. Since then, adherents of religions too numerous to name have made the United States their home, as have those whose beliefs expressly exclude religion. Precisely because of the religious diversity . . . the Founders added . . . a Bill of Rights, the very first words of which declare: "Congress shall make no law respecting an establishment of religion, or prohibiting the free exercise thereof." Perhaps in the early days of the Republic these words were understood to protect only the diversity within Christianity, but today they are recognized as guaranteeing religious liberty and equality to the infidel, the atheist, or the adherent of a non-Christian faith such as Islam or Judaism. . . . It is settled law that no government official in this Nation may violate these fundamental constitutional rights regarding matters of conscience.

This sets the stage by giving great weight to religious pluralism and the need to safeguard everyone's religious free exercise.

Justice Blackmun then goes on to a lengthy discussion of how the crèche scene violates the Establishment Clause because it so obviously suggests governmental endorsement of Christianity. But it is just as clear that he also regards such an endorsement as violating the Free Exercise Clause, because it communicates to non-Christians that their religions are *not* endorsed.

Justice Kennedy, joined by Chief Justice Rehnquist and Justices White and Scalia, offers several counterarguments, but the one of interest here is the claim that, in failing to accommodate the crèche scene in a government building, the majority opinion misinterprets the Establishment Clause:

> Rather than requiring government to avoid any action that acknowledges or aids religion, the Establishment Clause permits government some latitude in recognizing and accommodating

the central role religion plays in our society. . . . Any approach less sensitive to our heritage would border on latent hostility toward religion, as it would require government in all its multifaceted roles to acknowledge only the secular, to the exclusion and so to the detriment of the religious. [The consequence is:] Those religions enjoying the largest following must be consigned to the status of least-favored faiths so as to avoid any possible risk of offending members of minority religions.

Blackmun rises to this bait and in so doing reveals how deeply embedded in free-exercise issues is this establishment case:

Although Justice Kennedy repeatedly accuses the Court of harboring a "latent hostility" . . . toward religion . . . nothing could be further from the truth. Justice Kennedy apparently has misperceived a respect for religious pluralism, a respect commanded by the Constitution, as hostility or indifference to religion. No misperception could be more antithetical to the values embodied in the Establishment Clause. . . . In his attempt to legitimize the display of the crèche . . . Justice Kennedy repeatedly characterizes it as "accommodation" of religion. But accommodation of religion, in order to be permitted under the Establishment Clause, must lift an identifiable burden *on the exercise of religion.* . . . One may agree with Justice Kennedy that the scope of accommodations permissible under the Establishment Clause is larger than the scope of accommodations mandated by the Free Exercise Clause. . . . But a category of "permissible accommodations of religion not required by the Free Exercise Clause" aids the crèche . . . not at all. Prohibiting the display of a crèche at this location . . . does not impose a burden on the practice of Christianity (except to the extent that some Christian sect seeks to be an officially approved religion), and therefore permitting the display is not an "accommodation" of religion in the conventional sense.

In his own words, Justice Blackmun is accusing Justice Kennedy of defending nonpreferentialism, or what Marvin Frankel called "crabbed demands for status, authority, and petty but maddening superordination" (1992: 639).

Three years after the *Allegheny* crèche decision, a similar issue came before the Supreme Court, and once again nonpreferentialism was debated—separationists versus accommodationists. What was being challenged in *Lee v. Weisman* (1992) was the practice in a Providence, Rhode Island, junior high school of inviting local clergy to offer prayer at graduation ceremonies. Splitting pretty much as they had in *Allegheny*, the justices declared 5–4 that such prayers are unconstitutional. This time the dissent was written by Justice Scalia, who reiterated the nonpreferentialist credo that "government policies of accommodation, acknowledgement, and support for religion are an accepted part of our political and cultural heritage." That raised the ire of Justice Souter to the point of writing a rebuttal as a majority-concurring opinion in *Lee v. Weisman*. Souter's claim:

> Since *Everson*, we have consistently held the [Establishment] Clause applicable no less to governmental acts favoring religion generally than to acts favoring one religion over others. Thus in *Engel v. Vitale* . . . (1962), we held that the public schools may not subject their students to readings of any prayer, however "denominationally neutral." . . . More recently, in *Wallace v. Jaffree* . . . (1985), we held that an Alabama moment-of-silence statute passed for the sole purpose of "returning voluntary prayer to public schools" . . . violated the Establishment Clause even though it did not encourage students to pray to any particular deity. We said that "when the underlying principle has been examined in the crucible of litigation, the Court has unambiguously concluded that the individual freedom of conscience protected by the First Amendment embraces the right to select any religious faith or none at all."

It seems that what strict separationists see clearly—that once conscience is accorded the same protection that religion receives, Establishment Clause cases necessarily involve free-exercise considerations—nonpreferentialists do not see. David A. J. Richards goes so far as to claim that this relationship was known, at least to some, from the very beginning of the Republic. Thomas Jefferson, he says (1986: 12),

> elaborates the underlying moral ideal of respect for conscience to indulge not only free exercise, but any form of religious qualification for civil rights or any compulsion of tax money

for support of religious beliefs, even one's own. Since Jefferson believes that the rights of conscience are inalienable rights . . . he regards any state financial or other support for the propagation of religious belief as tyranny.

Actually, according to James Washington (1992: 21–21), while most of Jefferson's colleagues would have agreed that the "rights of conscience" are natural and inalienable, "this did not forestall nearly 150 years of theological and philosophical debates about the meaning of this phrase." While the debates go on, therefore, and the role of conscience is by no means fixed in law, Howe's "radical principle of liberty" does seem to be emerging as the free-exercise implications found in establishment cases are recognized, as are the establishment implications found in free-exercise cases. Granted, it has taken a long time to understand that when, say, a crèche scene is supported by tax money it is not just non-Christian believers whose truly free exercise of religion is being limited; also limited is the truly free exercise of Christian believers who observe their government sponsoring—however gently—*how* their Christianity is to be conceived and practiced. And that, as Jefferson would say, is "tyranny."

So far, we have argued that the expanded understanding of what is protected by the Free Exercise Clause and what is prohibited by the Establishment Clause represents the gradual unfolding of the true meaning and purpose of the First Amendment. That process took place very slowly from 1791 until 1940 because the Constitution restricted the power of the federal government to intervene on behalf of citizens against state laws. The Fourteenth Amendment, ratified in 1868, gave the federal government power to intervene when state laws infringed upon citizens' life, liberty, and property rights, but it was not until 1940, in *Cantwell v. Connecticut*, that the Supreme Court determined that religious free exercise was among those "liberty rights." The process of expanding religious liberty gained momentum after 1940, as the Supreme Court decided a series of church-state cases. As we have shown in this chapter, through this series of First Amendment challenges, the Court came to realize (1) that what the Free Exercise Clause of the First Amendment protects is the freedom of conscience, whether conscience is expressed in religious or secular terms (2) because to make the distinction between religious and secular expressions of conscience would mire the Court in the task of defining religion; this (3) would require the Court to judge the truth of religious opinions, which (4) would necessarily be an unconstitutional establishment of religion.

As the cases we have reviewed here show, the expanded understanding of what may be freely exercised necessarily meant further restriction of the government's authority to act in matters of conscience. The question then became one of defining the circumstances under which the government might legitimately act in matters where conscience is concerned. In *Sherbert* the Court answered that the government could act when (1) it had a compelling and legitimate interest at stake and (2) there was no way to advance that interest without burdening the religious liberty rights of citizens. While there could certainly be disagreement about what constituted a compelling and legitimate interest, and thus application of these tests did not automatically render decisions, the Sherbert test provided a useful barrier against the arbitrary use of the coercive powers of government to advance or impede conscientiously motivated behavior, even while it allowed the state to intervene when conscientiously motivated behavior threatened public safety or imposed on the rights of others.

Conclusion

It took very little time, as we saw in chapter 3, for Joseph Story and others to misunderstand the design for true religious liberty envisioned by the Founders. Indeed, for a century and a half the only progress toward the Founders' ideal was the emergence of what is now called nonpreferentialism—a recognition that government may not interfere (except under stipulated circumstances) in the free exercise of any generally recognized religion, nor may it favor or disfavor any one or more expressions of such a religion.

The next step toward the properly understood constitutional requirement regarding church and state was, by contrast, quite rapid. Beginning in 1940 in *Cantwell v. Connecticut*, the process unfolded in a mere twenty-five years, reaching its apogee in 1965 in *United States v. Seeger*. As we have seen earlier, in this case the Supreme Court recognized that what the Free Exercise Clause protects is conscience, and with that recognition came the realization that the Establishment Clause *also* needs to be reinterpreted. Why this is so is illustrated in the next chapter, with three case studies: abortion, euthanasia, and same-sex marriage. Chapter 7 then concludes our argument by discussing how this constitutionally protected position of conscience is under assault and why.

Notes

1. Some of the material in this chapter was published in Phillip E. Hammond, *With Liberty for All* (Louisville, Ky.: Westminster John Knox Press, 1998).
2. This argument is variously addressed in Carmela 1993, Davis 1993, Frankel 1994, Galanter 1966, Greenawalt 1993, Ingber 1989, and Lerner 1989.

6

Three Case Studies[1]

Just as, for Madison, the freedom of religion led inevitably to disestablishment as discussed in chapter 2, we demonstrated in chapter 5 that once conscience was recognized as the equivalent of religion, and thus what may be freely exercised, this led inevitably toward a greater separation of church and state. Circumstances in which the state was seen to be privileging religious over nonreligious perspectives could now be challenged as unconstitutional establishments of religion. Expanded free exercise meant more restriction on government sponsorship of religion. But this jurisprudence led naturally to certain conclusions that unsettled religious conservatives. In particular, they objected to Court decisions that ruled unconstitutional state-sponsored school prayer and devotional Bible reading. While conservatives might have applauded decisions that expanded religious free exercise, they objected to the natural corollary of such expansion, the rooting out of unconstitutional establishment/nonpreferentialism.

Conservatives are even more alarmed by what expanded free exercise means for issues such as abortion, euthanasia, and homosexual rights. These issues do not concern *religious* free exercise—no one is arguing that their religion compelled them to terminate pregnancies, to end the lives of persons suffering with terminal diseases, or to engage in homosexual conduct—but these are clearly issues that involve the exercise of *conscience*. The trend toward expanded liberty of conscience has led logically to greater moral autonomy for individuals and further restrictions on the government's ability to regulate such behaviors.

The First Amendment challenge so far to laws restricting abortion, medical assistance for suicide, and homosexual behavior has made only limited progress, but a brief examination of these issues suggests that the challenge has gained momentum and may continue to do so unless the forces discussed in the next chapter prevail.

Abortion

In 1979, the U.S. Supreme Court, by a vote of 5–4 in *Harris v. McRae*, upheld the constitutionality of the congressional legislation known as the Hyde Amendment, which prohibits federal funding for Medicaid abortions. Cora McRae, a pregnant indigent woman eligible for Medicaid, desired an abortion for therapeutic reasons but was turned down. She brought suit on several grounds: that she was denied due process and that both the Establishment Clause and the Free Exercise Clause were violated in her case. The majority rejected all three of these claims. McRae's due process was not violated, the majority said, because she was not denied abortion, only the federal funds to pay for it. The claim based on the Establishment Clause was rejected because, while some religions do regard abortion as sinful, that fact does not prevent government from passing laws outlawing abortion. Finally, McRae's Free Exercise argument was rejected because she did not allege, let alone prove, that she sought an abortion "under compulsion of religious belief."

The four dissenters in this case, however, had a markedly different picture of the issue. It is not far-fetched to suggest that, contrary to the majority view, McRae's free exercise of religion *was* violated, at least if "conscience" is what can be freely exercised. This perspective is clear in the dissent of Justice Brennan:

> My focus . . . is upon the coercive impact of the congressional decision to fund one outcome of pregnancy—childbirth—while not funding the other—abortion. . . . [T]he Hyde Amendment is a transparent attempt by the Legislative Branch to impose the

political majority's judgment of the morally acceptable and socially desirable preference on a sensitive and intimate decision that the Constitution entrusts to the individual.

Might Brennan have been comfortable tacking the word "conscience" onto that last sentence? Obviously, we do not know how Justice Brennan would respond to our hypothetical question, but further on in Brennan's dissent he draws a parallel between McRae and Seventh-Day Adventist Sherbert, who was denied unemployment compensation by the state when she resigned her job rather than work on Saturdays. Brennan quotes from the majority opinion that he himself wrote in that case (*Sherbert v. Verner*, 1963):

> The ruling [denying her benefits] forces her to choose between following the precepts of her religion and forfeiting benefits, on the one hand, and abandoning one of the precepts of her religion in order to accept work, on the other hand. Governmental imposition of such a choice puts the same kind of burden upon the free exercise of religion as would a fine imposed against appellant for her Saturday worship.

We are *not* suggesting that McRae's free exercise of religion (in the narrow sense) was assaulted by the Hyde Amendment; we *are* suggesting that the Hyde Amendment represents an unconstitutional establishment of one conscientious position over alternative conscientious positions—which violates McRae's freedom of conscience and thus the Free Exercise Clause as interpreted here. Justice Brennan seems to have recognized this implication in the case.

This interpretation is more clearly illustrated in another abortion case nine years later, *Webster v. Reproductive Health Services*. The same four justices dissented, but it is Justice Stevens's dissent we attend to here. *Webster* resulted from a certain Missouri legislative bill, the preamble of which declared that the life of "each human being begins at conception." Three other provisions stipulated certain regulations to be followed in abortion cases: that no public funds be used to encourage abortion, that no public employees or facilities be used in performing abortions, and that a viability test be performed on the fetus of any woman seeking abortion if reason exists to believe she is twenty or more weeks pregnant.

Justice Stevens is bothered chiefly by the preamble. He writes:

> I am persuaded that the absence of any secular purpose for the legislative declaration that life begins at conception and that conception occurs at fertilization makes the relevant portion of the preamble invalid under the Establishment Clause. . . . This conclusion does not, and could not, rest on the fact that the statement happens to coincide with the tenets of certain religions . . . or on the fact that the legislators who voted to enact it may have been motivated by religious considerations. . . . Rather, it rests on the fact that the preamble, an unequivocal endorsement of a religious tenet of some but by no means all . . . faiths, serves no identifiable secular purpose. That fact alone compels a conclusion that the statute violates the Establishment Clause.

And, we would add, because the law restricts women's ability to act according to the dictates of their own conscience, it also violates the Free Exercise Clause.

It is important to note that Justice Stevens is not choosing secularism over religion. He is not stating that life does *not* begin at conception. Rather, he is saying that whether or not life begins at conception is necessarily a conscience issue, not because religions have views on this issue but because the state had no compelling interest in declaring that life begins at conception. Even if the pro-choice supporters in this case did not regard their position as "religious," that position was conscientiously held and therefore, in Justice Stevens's view, entitled to the same First Amendment protection enjoyed by their opponents—the right to "select any religious faith or none at all."

Is it possible, we can ask, to believe profoundly that abortion is evil and still leave the decision to abort to the pregnant woman whose life and conscience is most directly connected to the choice? That pair of views, writes Ronald Dworkin (1993: 15), "is not only consistent but is in keeping with a great tradition of freedom of conscience in modern pluralistic democracies." What is really at issue in abortion cases, Dworkin insists (1993: 25–26), is whether state legislatures have the constitutional power to decide which intrinsic value all citizens must respect, and how, and whether legislatures may prohibit abortion on that ground. . . . [F]*reedom of choice about abortion is a necessary implication of the religious freedom guaranteed by the First Amendment* [emphasis added].[2]

David A. J. Richards makes the case more generally. The moral basis of the Free Exercise Clause, he writes, is "immunizing from state coercion the exercise of conceptions of life well and ethically lived and expressive of a mature person's rational and reasonable powers." Likewise, the Establishment Clause prohibits the state from interfering with the "forming and changing of those conceptions" (1986: 140).

Euthanasia

As has often been noted, the legal and moral issues involved in assisted suicide are much the same as those in the case of abortion. As a Ninth Circuit Federal Court decision regarding assisted suicide recently stated, "[B]oth types of case raise issues of life and death, and both arouse similar religious and moral concerns. Both also present basic questions about an individual's right of choice" (*Compassion in Dying v. State of Washington*, 1996).

As in the case of abortion, the significant issue is this: On what basis may the state restrict an individual's right of choice? The first case we examine (*Cruzan v. Director, Missouri Department of Health*, 1990) involved a Missouri law that required "clear and convincing evidence" of an incompetent, terminally ill person's wish to have life-sustaining treatment withdrawn before any such withdrawal could be approved. Nancy Cruzan was a victim of an auto accident that had left her for six years in a "permanent vegetative state." The testimony of her parents and her one-time housemate, that Nancy often expressed her desire to avoid being kept alive by such means, was found insufficient by a lower court, and a five-person majority of the Missouri Supreme Court could find no constitutional basis for finding otherwise. The Supreme Court upheld the decision of the Missouri court, but as in other cases we are examining here the jurisprudence we are identifying is found not in the majority opinion but in the dissent. It is, of course, no coincidence that the dissenters in this case are the four whose views we have already encountered—Brennan, Blackmun, Marshall, and Stevens. In *Cruzan* it is Stevens's dissent that best illustrates our argument:

> [N]ot much may be said with confidence about death unless it is said from faith, and that alone is reason enough to protect the freedom to conform choices about death to individual conscience. . . . Missouri asserts that its policy is related to a state interest in the protection of life. In my view, however, it is an effort to define life, rather than to protect it, that is the heart of Missouri's policy. Missouri insists, without regard to Nancy Cruzan's own interests, upon equaling her life with the biological persistence of her bodily functions. . . . [T]here is a serious question as to whether the mere persistence of their bodies is "life" as that word is commonly understood, or as it is used in both the Constitution and the Declaration of Independence. . . . It is not within the province of secular government to circumscribe the liberties of the people by regulations designed wholly for the purpose of *establishing a sectarian definition of life* [emphasis added].

It is hardly surprising that in this dissent Justice Stevens footnotes his earlier dissent in the *Webster* abortion case. In both cases, he sees legislation that arbitrarily defines life—when it begins in *Webster*, when it ends in *Cruzan*—the effect each time being the unnecessary and unconstitutional establishment of an ultimate perspective not shared by all. If not an establishment of religion in the narrow sense, it *is* an establishment of one conscientious position, disregarding—even outlawing—alternative conscientious positions. That is what Justice Stevens objects to.

In 1996 the Ninth Circuit Court of Appeals declared unconstitutional the Washington State law making a felony of any physician-assisted suicide (*Compassion in Dying v. State of Washington*). The Ninth Circuit was mindful of the seriousness of the case before them. A lower court had found for the plaintiffs in 1994. Upon a first appeal to the Ninth Circuit, that judgment was reversed 2 to 1, which led to an 11-judge panel that reheard the case and affirmed the lower court's ruling. After laying out the circumstances of the case, the majority strikes the seriousness note:

> There is no litmus test for courts to apply when deciding whether or not a liberty interest exists under the Due Process Clause. Our decisions involve difficult judgments regarding the conscience, traditions, and fundamental tenets of our nation. We must sometimes apply those basic principles in light of changing values based on shared experience. Other times we must apply them to new problems arising out of the development and use of new technologies. In all cases, our analysis of the applicability of the protections of the Constitution must be made in light of existing circumstances as well as our historic traditions.

The Ninth Circuit Court then reviewed a great many cases from the past in which "personal" matters have been adjudicated, deciding that "few decisions arc more personal, intimate or important than the decision to end one's life, especially when the reason for doing so is to avoid excessive and protracted pain." It then quotes from a 1992 Supreme Court decision (*Planned Parenthood v. Casey*):

> The most intimate and personal choices a person may make in a lifetime, choices central to personal dignity and autonomy, are central to the liberty protected by the Fourteenth Amendment. At the heart of liberty is the right to define one's own concept of existence, of meaning, of the universe, and of the mystery of human life. Beliefs about these matters could not define the attributes of personhood were they formed under compulsion of the State.

On this basis, then, the Ninth Circuit Court in this assisted suicide case wrote the summary statement so widely quoted in news stories about this case:

> A competent terminally ill adult, having lived nearly the full measure of his life, has a strong liberty interest in choosing a dignified and humane death rather than being reduced at the end of his existence to a childlike state of helplessness, diapered, sedated, incontinent.

That summary statement does not highlight the relevance this case has for our purposes, however. What does this is the decisions' concluding paragraph:

> There is one final point we must emphasize. Some argue strongly that decisions regarding matters affecting life or death should not be made by the courts. Essentially, we agree with that proposition. In this case, by permitting the individual to exercise the right to choose we are following the constitutional mandate to take such decisions out of the hands of the government, both state and federal, and to put them where they rightly belong, in the hands of the people. We are allowing individuals to make the decisions that so profoundly affect their very existence—and precluding the state from intruding excessively into that critical realm. . . . Those who believe strongly that death must come without physician assistance are free to follow that creed, be they doctors or patients. *They are not free, however, to force their views, their religious convictions, or their philosophies on all the other members of a democratic society, and to compel those whose values differ with theirs to die painful, protracted and agonizing deaths* [emphasis added].

The vote was 8–3, which, along with the fact that this appellate case challenges the *Cruzan* decision, probably destined it to go to the U.S. Supreme Court. Indeed, in October 1996 the Court agreed to hear the appeal, joining the Ninth Circuit decision to a similar decision arising in the Second Circuit. Oral arguments were heard in January 1997, and the following June the Court overturned both circuit courts' decisions (*Washington et al. v. Glucksberg et al.* and *Vacco et al. v. Quill et al.*).

The reasoning of the Ninth Circuit Court was rejected—unanimously—by the Supreme Court. Chief Justice Rehnquist wrote the opinion, joined by four other justices. The remaining four, while concurring in the outcome, make two points in their opinion. First, they note that laws now permit physicians to prescribe drugs for patients sufficient to control pain, despite the risk that those drugs themselves will kill. Second, however, in rejecting the claims made by the states of Washington and New York, these four justices recognize that there are grounds for finding "a right to die with dignity" (Justice Breyer, concurring opinion in the two cases). Justice Stevens is even more outspoken:

> A State, like Washington, that has authorized the death penalty and thereby has concluded that the sanctity of human life does not require that it always be preserved, must acknowledge that there are situations in which an interest in hastening death is legitimate. Indeed, not only is that interest sometimes legitimate, I am also convinced that there are times when it is entitled to constitutional protection.

The "liberty interest" Justice Stevens identified in *Cruzan* remains real for him at least. In the meantime, these two cases have upheld the right of states to outlaw assisted suicide; what they don't do is prohibit states from changing their laws to permit assisted suicide—in accordance with what polls show the public desires by a margin of 5 to 4. Certainly the cases that arose in Washington and New York are not the end of this issue. If the analysis here is correct, the eventual outcome is predictable.

Homosexuality

Only recently has homosexuality joined this company of issues. The Georgia sodomy case (*Bowers v. Hardwick*, 1985) was technically not a decision about same-sex activity, since heterosexual sodomy was also outlawed by the Georgia statute, but it nonetheless stands as a measure of Supreme Court thinking less than two decades ago. The majority voted to uphold the Georgia statute, while the dissenters saw that Georgia was imposing a sectarian moral viewpoint. Indeed, Justice Lewis Powell, who voted with the majority, is reported to have said, after he retired, that he had voted wrongly. The legal standing of homosexuality is obviously "ripening" as gay and lesbian persons are insisting on their rights as citizens, including the right to marry. As with abortion and euthanasia, these demands touch on the very core of what "conscience" means.

In his book *The Case for Same-Sex Marriage*, William N. Eskridge Jr., makes the case that existing state policies unconstitutionally discriminate when they pick and choose, rather arbitrarily, which citizens should enjoy a right that the courts have determined to be fundamentally linked to political citizenship:

> Wisconsin's marriage statute codifies the understanding of marriage that recurs in the case law: "Marriage is the institution that is the foundation of family and society. Its stability is basic to morality and civilization, and of vital interest to society and the state." Consistent with this philosophy, the states are not discriminating about who can partake of this institution. It is open to any consenting nonrelated couple—except lesbian or gay couples. . . . [N]o state refuses to issue a marriage license to a couple on the ground that society disapproves of their erotic practices or their sexual orientation—unless they are homosexual. The state will issue a marriage license to sadists, masochists, transvestites, and fetishists, so long as they are heterosexual sadists, masochists, transvestites, and fetishists. . . . [T]he pedophile (someone who is sexually attracted to minors) can also get a marriage license, so long as he or she is a heterosexual pedophile and is willing to go to some trouble. (Eskridge 1996: 63–64)

The implication of the pattern drawn by Eskridge is clear: The right of marriage is so fundamental that it is protected by the courts for murderers, pedophiles, and rapists. Only homosexuals must "sit at the back of the bus" (1996: 65).

As with the argument for legal abortion and legal euthanasia, Eskridge rests his claims for same-sex marriage on the Due Process and Equal Protection Clauses of the U.S. Constitution's Fourteenth Amendment; this is a "liberty" right, not a "free exercise of religion" right he is discussing. We contend that, in the absence of compelling state interest and/or secular purpose, homosexual rights—like abortion rights and euthanasia rights—reflect the rights of conscience.

The free conscience argument for gay rights has been presented forcefully by Richards (1999). The denial of marriage and other rights solely on the basis of sexual orientation amounts to what Richards calls "moral slavery," which is characterized by two features: "First, abridgment of basic human rights to a group of persons; and second, the unjust rationalization of such abridgement on the inadequate grounds of dehumanizing stereotypes" (53). The unconstitutional logic of legal discrimination against homosexuals, in Richards's view, goes something like this: Homosexuality involves a moral choice. Because homosexuals make what some people perceive to be the wrong choice, they are deemed incapable of exercising moral judgment. Since homosexuals are seen as incapable of exercising moral judgment, the state considers itself justified in restricting their moral autonomy.

At stake is not only the right to marry, to be free from discrimination in employment and housing, and so on, but also, and more important, the right to the free exercise of conscience. To make some behavior illegal solely on the grounds that a powerful group in society finds it morally objectionable is to deprive dissenters of the freedom to exercise moral judgment. The evil of such institutionalized prejudice is, again in Richards's words, "its unjust abridgment of the inalienable right to conscience, the free exercise of the moral powers of rationality and reasonableness in terms of which persons define personal and ethical meaning in living" (1999: 86). It is, in other words, an unjust abridgment of the very rights protected by the First Amendment.

A preliminary view of the power of such an argument to secure gay and lesbian rights may be found in a case that overturned Colorado's Amendment Two (*Romer v. Evans*, 1996). The amendment attempted to ban all laws that recognized antidiscrimination claims by gays and lesbians. According to Richards, "Its aim was decisively that advocates of gay and lesbian identity should be compelled to abandon their claims to personal and moral legitimacy and either convert to the true view or return to the silence of their traditional unspeakability" (1999: 92). Both sides could agree that the expression of gay or lesbian identity is a moral choice. However, "the opposition (on sectarian religious grounds) interprets the choice as a moral heresy, [while] its advocates construe the choice as an exercise of legitimate moral freedom" (92). The underlying issue, as decided by the courts, is not whether the gay and lesbian claim to moral legitimacy is right or wrong, but rather whether or not the law may restrict the freedom of individual citizens to make the moral choice and to defend that choice in the public realm. The amendment to Colorado's constitution, therefore, infringed on both the free exercise of conscience and the freedom of public dissent—a clear violation of the First Amendment, although this was not the basis of the Court's decision.

In June 2003, the Supreme Court overturned *Bowers v. Hardwick* on the grounds that antisodomy laws violated homosexuals' liberty rights as guaranteed by the Fourteenth Amendment (*Lawrence et al. v. Texas*). Although the three dissenters in the case—Rehnquist, Scalia, and Thomas—adamantly refused to acknowledge it, the majority opinion, written by Justice Kennedy, makes clear that the liberty right at stake is not a right to engage in sodomy, but a right to privacy and to moral autonomy. Kennedy makes this explicit in the opening paragraph of the majority opinion:

> Liberty protects the person from unwarranted government intrusions into a dwelling or other private places. In our tradition the State is not omnipresent in the home. And there are other spheres of our lives and existence, outside the home, where the State should not be a dominant presence. . . . *Liberty presumes an autonomy of self that includes the freedom of thought, belief, expression, and certain intimate conduct.* (emphasis added)

Echoing the Sherbert test, Kennedy applies a "rational purpose" standard to the antisodomy law, which acknowledges that there are times when the government may restrict individual autonomy, but only when there is a compelling interest at stake, such as "injury to a person or abuse of an institution the law protects." Imposing a sectarian moral code, however, does not meet that standard:

> [F]or centuries there have been powerful voices to condemn homosexual conduct as immoral. The condemnation has been shaped by religious beliefs, conceptions of right and acceptable behavior, and respect for the traditional family. For many persons these are not trivial concerns but profound and deep convictions accepted as ethical and moral principles to which they

aspire and which thus determine the course of their lives. These considerations do not answer the question before us, however. The issue is whether the majority may use the power of the State to enforce these views on the whole society through operation of the criminal laws.

He then quotes the Court's opinion in *Planned Parenthood of Southeastern Pa. v. Casey* (1992): "Our obligation is to determine the liberty of all, not to mandate our own moral code."

Conservative voices exclaimed that the *Lawrence* decision signaled "the end of morality legislation." So, we would argue, it ought to be because in a society that respects the freedom of conscience the government has no business dictating morality. Whether homosexuality is moral or immoral in an absolute sense is not a matter for legislatures or courts to decide. Instead, the mandate of the Courts is to protect the right of the individual to make moral assessments, unless the state can demonstrate some compelling interest in the outcome of such assessments. Even if the conclusions reached by the individual are wrong, in matters of conscience the First Amendment protects the right to err unless that error leads to some demonstrable harm. Indeed, from the perspective developed here, the freedom to make only what some people believe to be the "correct" assessment of religious and moral matters would be no freedom at all.

Conclusion

The guidelines established in *Sherbert* for balancing the legitimate interests of government in maintaining social order against the freedom of religion guaranteed in the First Amendment could be readily applied to these and similar matters of conscience, and if applied would lead to the conclusion that, in the words of Peter Wenz (1992: 25):

> The value of democracy rests . . . on the values of peace and of equal respect for people and for their powers of self-determination. . . . But respect for the value of individual self-determination cannot be maintained by submitting all matters to a democratic

vote. Democracy is required only in situations where people depend on others with whom they cannot realistically negotiate a private accord. Where people are independent of one another, or can protect their interests through private negotiations without jeopardizing the interests of others, the value of self-determination is best served by allowing adults to act as they choose.

Or, to paraphrase Madison, Jefferson, and the Supreme Court in *Sherbert*, people should be free to act according to the dictates of their own conscience so long as, in doing so, they do not harm the rights of others or imperil the public safety.

Liberal-minded Americans have applauded these trends. Conservatives, however, take a very different view. They see decisions outlawing state-sponsored school prayer and devotional Bible reading but allowing abortion and possibly physician-assisted suicide and homosexual rights as evidence that the government has become hostile to religion and friendly to "secular humanism" and moral depravity. This view, however, turns the issue upside down. It imposes one moral order on other people without any constitutional justification. Neither the state nor an individual can seek to pass laws reflecting a moral position, binding on all, unless one or both of the following two conditions are met: (1) Empirical evidence supports incontrovertibly one side of the issue over the other side. Thus Christian Science parents must provide medical services for their sick children because the evidence is clear that doing so saves lives, and the state has a duty to protect life. Laws against murder, rape, theft, and the like fall into this category. (2) Reason or logic underlies many laws demanding conformity, not because empirical evidence supports them but because reasonable people can see the wisdom of such laws. Thus churches must be constructed in conformity with the building code for the same reason that driving on only one side of the road is required.

Laws outlawing abortion *on the grounds that life begins at conception* meet neither of these criteria. Nor does a law that states life still exists as long as machines keep bodily functions going. And what empirical evidence or logic supports the idea that two people of the same sex cannot form a legally binding union? As

Justice Kennedy wrote (quoted above) "Liberty presumes an autonomy of self that includes freedom of thought, belief, expression, and certain intimate conduct."

Where conservatives see favoritism for "secular humanism" and moral depravity, we see even-handed enlightenment, liberty, and protection of conscience. Our view, however, is under assault, with significant support already on the Supreme Court of the United States. We turn finally to the battle now underway in the Supreme Court.

Notes

1. Portions of this chapter are drawn, with permission, from Phillip E. Hammond, *With Liberty for All* (Louisville, Ky.: Westminster John Knox Press, 1998); from David W. Machacek, "Religion and Sexual Liberty: Personal versus Civic Morality in America," in *Sexuality and the World's Religions*, ed. D. W. Machacek and M. M. Wilcox (Santa Barbara, Calif.: ABC-CLIO, 2003), 359–84.

2. Peter Wenz makes the same argument in his book *Abortion Rights as Religious Freedom* (1992).

7

Regression on the Court: Religious Freedom on Trial[1]

The 1980 election of Ronald Reagan marked the return to power of the conservatives, which, like the liberals' triumphs of the 1930–1968 period, involves the Supreme Court, and within it the matter of church-state separation. Reagan, beyond standing for the virtues of big business and small government traditionally associated with the Republican Party, charged America with moral decline, which brought evangelical Christians into the Republican camp. Reagan won big, and the conservative movement reached a strength not unlike that of the Great Society in LBJ's first years. Conservatism has dominated America from 1980 to the present, a situation that eight years of Bill Clinton did little to change.

The solidification of conservatism means that America has two ideological camps, each with roots many decades old. American politics now offers a picture of heightened partisanship. Presidential politics is the more volatile branch, of course, exhibited in the Nixon election in a "liberal" climate and the Clinton election in a "conservative" climate. Congress is more stable over time, the Senate more so than the House of Representatives. That leaves the U.S. Supreme Court the least volatile of the three branches of the American government, largely because justices serve for life, easily outlasting the power of the presidents and senators who put them in office. There is, moreover, another constraint on volatility in the Supreme Court, a constraint not imposing on the legislative and executive branches. It is this: Not only are precedents respected, but the judicial branch's very task is to interpret a document—the U.S. Constitution—which is the governmental plan for organizing a society in a way that makes possible the pursuit of the goals set forth in the Declaration of Independence. The Constitution is thus regarded as "unchangeable," though how it is interpreted of course changes over time. The question of how, even whether, such changes can occur is a matter of profound philosophical difference, as we shall see.

When Progressive Liberalism Prevailed

William H. Rehnquist, fresh out of Stanford Law School, was a law clerk for Associate Justice Robert H. Jackson in 1952 and 1953. During this time, the U.S. Supreme Court heard and decided *Brown v. Board of Education*, which declared unconstitutional the practice of racial segregation in public schools. Rehnquist wrote a memo on the *Brown* case in which he claimed that the Court was "being asked to read its own sociological views into the Constitution" and to adopt a position "palpably at variance with precedent and probably with legislative history." Rehnquist then added, "If this Court, because its members individually are 'liberal' and dislike segregation, now chooses to strike it down, it differs from the McReynolds Court only in the kinds of litigants it favors and the kinds of special claims it protects" (quoted in Taylor 2002: 42).

By "the McReynolds Court" Rehnquist was, of course, referring to the bloc of Supreme Court justices who, until 1937, found unconstitutional much of Roosevelt's New Deal legislation designed to respond to the Great Depression. However, between 1937 and 1939, Roosevelt was able to replace four justices on the Court, and a new understanding of the U.S. Constitution was the result. Rehnquist quite properly notes the enormous difference between the pre-1937 Court and the Court since.

The election of Franklin Delano Roosevelt to the U.S. presidency in 1932 set in motion a great number of changes that revolutionized American society. Indeed, the argument can be made that the revolution carried over to the Lyndon B. Johnson years, notably with the passage of both the Civil Rights and War-on-Poverty bills. By this time, of course, Richard Nixon had served five years in the White House and Gerald Ford three, but neither did much to dismantle the New Deal programs. Earlier, Dwight Eisenhower, in his eight years in office (1953–1961) did even less. In fact, William F. Buckley, already an articulate spokesman for the conservative cause, denounced Eisenhower in a 1956 editorial, claiming that Ike's first term had been marked by "easy and wholehearted acceptance" of "measured socialism"(1956: 6–7. Barry Goldwater's defeat in 1964 by the largest margin in a presidential vote in American history is further testimony to the settled acceptance of New Deal–type programs by the majority of American voters, though Goldwater's militant reputation no doubt also worked against him, given the fears of an expanding war in Vietnam.

Although Nixon's election in 1968 evidenced a growing conservative mood in the electorate, Johnson's quagmire in Vietnam probably did more for Nixon's victory than a not-yet-very-active conservative movement. Nixon was not a conservative in the Buckley mold, let alone sympathetic with tax revolters and the Christian Right, who were yet to become vocal and visible.

What were the New Deal programs that were so favored during these decades? They included emergency relief for the unemployed, bank reform, stock exchange regulations, Social Security, the Wagner Act regarding labor relations, broadened international trade, and the practice of "pump-priming" the economy, à la John Maynard Keynes.[2] It is true that FDR had his enemies, but the New Deal prevailed. Progressive legislation was enacted by the Congress and upheld by a progressive Supreme Court. As Jerome Himmelstein (1990: 19) writes about both the House and the Senate in 1938, opposition to the New Deal

> remained weak and disorganized. The Republican party was a small minority . . . and lacked clear leadership. The nascent conservative coalition in Congress never fully solidified; its support shifted from issue to issue and fell apart totally in such areas as farm legislation.

New Deal programs in general can be seen as expansions of individual freedom—recognizing people's right to economic security in old age, laborers' right to unionize, bank customers' right to have safe money accounts, and so on. This expansion of individual freedom also occurred in the area of religion, though in a quite different manner. It was the action not of the Congress but of the Supreme Court, and this expansion began in 1940 in a case we discussed in chapter 5, *Cantwell v. Connecticut.*

In chapter 5, we pointed out that *Cantwell* served as a trigger for two ensuing decisions: *which* religious motivations are constitutionally protected, and what is *truly* religious? But *Cantwell* was also the case in which the U.S. Supreme Court incorporated the Free Exercise Clause into the Fourteenth Amendment. The Fourteenth Amendment forbids the states from depriving their citizens of liberty without due process of law. Ratified in 1868 for the purpose of giving the federal government the power to declare illegal state laws permitting slavery, later Courts interpreted the Fourteenth Amendment as giving the Supreme Court jurisdiction to strike down, with due process, state laws that violated rights protected by the U.S. Constitution. Prior to this shift in jurisprudence, the guarantees of liberty declared in the Bill of Rights were understood only to restrict actions by the federal government (although, as we saw in chapter 4, that understanding was beginning to change even before 1868). Except in rare circumstances, challenges to state laws were referred to state courts to be decided according to their respective legislation or state constitutions. For citizens living in states whose constitutions provided only weak protection for rights, this system provided little or no protection against unjust laws, and slavery, which was legal in some states and illegal in others, was a most egregious case in point. The Thirteenth Amendment did away with slavery in America, but the Fourteenth Amendment empowered the federal government to expand liberty in accordance with the standards of the U.S. Constitution.

As later Courts perceived, the implications of the Fourteenth Amendment extended far beyond the issue of slavery. Now, state laws concerning the establishment of religion or its free exercise, state laws concerning the freedom of speech, the press, and association, and state laws concerning the possession of firearms, among a host of other issues concerning the rights of American citizens could be adjudicated according to federal principles. As we noted in chapters 3 and 4, passage of the Fourteenth Amendment, therefore, signals the beginning of a dramatic shift in the relationship between the state and national governments, one which led to a greatly expanded role for the national government and a decline in the sovereignty of the individual state governments. Needless to say, many conservatives today detest this development.

Some other rights enumerated in the Bill of Rights had already been incorporated, but the incorporation of the Free Exercise Clause in *Cantwell* and the incorporation of the Establishment Clause in *Everson v. Board of Education* in 1947 meant that the U.S. Supreme Court would hear and decide many more church-state cases than it had before 1940. This increase was significant. As already reported, the U.S. Supreme Court decided few religion cases from 1845 through 1939. Between 1940 and 2002, it decided 88, sometimes 3 or 4 in a single year. The Court, in other words, now plays a much larger role in American church-state policies, just as, after 1937 it played a much larger role in American economic, medical, regulatory, and educational realms.

Though interrupted by World War II, the New Deal's civilian program was the federal government's way of mitigating the misfortunes accompanying industrialization, a cause that had long been recognized but responded to inadequately. The campaign continued after the war with such projects as rural electrification, the GI Bill, interstate highway construction, a minimum wage law, Medicare, and so on. Altogether, then, at the time of Nixon's 1968 election, Americans could look back and see the triumph of collective welfare over unregulated free markets, federalism over states' rights, internationalism over isolationism, and an activist Court over a passive Court. Regarding this last change, Morton Horowitz writes: "The New Deal constitutional revolution of 1937 represented a fundamental shift in the constitutional relationship of the states to the federal government as well as of government to the economy" (1992: 3).[3] As we have seen, the "constitutional revolution" to which Horowitz refers also represents a fundamental shift in the relationship of government to matters of church and state.

This constitutional revolution is crucial to the story here, because while some in the conservative movement that was to follow objected to all of these New Deal/Great Society changes, all in that movement objected to some, and none of these changes evoked more emotional vehemence than the church-state decisions of the Earl Warren Court. All over America, but especially in the South, billboards and bumper stickers urged "Impeach Earl Warren." Appointed by President Eisenhower in 1953 and serving as chief justice for the next sixteen years, Warren and his Court embodied for liberals much that was good in America but for conservatives much that was bad.

One notable controversy followed the Warren Court's two decisions in 1962 and 1963 that declared unconstitutional school-sponsored prayer and devotional Bible reading. Only Associate Justice Potter Stewart dissented, but the public reaction split along much the same line as the reaction to other progressive programs. A progressive Court and most liberal-minded Americans saw the decisions as expanding the separation of church and state, thereby allowing more religious freedom and less government dictation of religious beliefs and practices. Put another way, these two decisions (and others yet to come) indicated how church-state issues were embedded in the ideological matrix we have called the New Deal/Great Society movement. Why? By being yet another expansion of liberty, in this case expanding people's freedom to be religious in the way they choose. Just as economic regulations expanded people's freedom from unjust market practices, so did Social Security provide a measure of freedom from poverty in old age, and school desegregation expanded the freedom of black American children to get a good education. Underlying all of these changes, and more, is the central idea of individual liberty, the freedom to follow one's conscience unless government has a compelling interest in restricting it.

Expanding people's freedom in these various ways always met with objections, but until the 1960s those objections tended to make little headway. That is no longer the case.

Regression Emerges

Beginning with the 1964 Barry Goldwater campaign, the Republican Party began to consolidate the various branches of conservatism in America. Today, it leads an ideological movement that is quite accurately described as "anti-New Deal/Great Society." This ideology showed up first in the presidency of Richard Nixon, intensified with the eight years of Ronald Reagan, and appears magnified under the second George Bush. The 2002 congressional election gave Republicans control of both houses of Congress, and the announced agenda involves more "un-doing" than "doing," and what is to be undone is much that has been created since 1937. This includes undoing some of what has expanded religious liberty. That agenda is not merely *conservative* (advocating the status quo or slow change), therefore, but *regressive* (advocating a reversal of progress already made toward greater individual freedom).

The judicial branch of government has been slowest to move to the right, in part because of the life-long tenure of Supreme Court justices, and in part because of the hold of precedent in the decision making of sitting justices. President George W. Bush has announced his intention to nominate candidates like Justices Antonin Scalia and Clarence Thomas, however, who along with Chief Justice Rehnquist make up the "regressive" core of the current Supreme Court. We think that this move, if it comes about, would be disastrous to religious freedom.

How the Supreme Court Fits in the Larger Political Picture

The question can be asked whether in this massive shift from the liberal 1932–1968 period to the conservative 1980-present period the U.S. Supreme Court was part of this shift. The answer of course is *Yes*, and it is evident in battles over church-state cases. We need merely equate regressivism with less "separation of church and state" and progressivism with more. When we do this equating, we see that the 1930–1968 period was clearly a period of expanding separation and thus greater religious liberty, and we see that since 1980 this expansion has slowed down and in certain respects is now being challenged. How do we know? By looking at how the justices vote on church-state issues.

In almost all church-state cases, justices are asked (1) to allow—on free-exercise grounds—what is not now allowed, or (2) to prohibit—on establishment grounds—what is now allowed. Affirmative votes in both types of cases are "separationist" votes, making it easy to "score" each justice and learn how inclined each is to keep and/or expand the separation of church and state in the United States.[4] On this basis the leading separationist title belongs to Justice William O. Douglas with a score of 100 percent, and the antiseparationist title belongs to Justice Clarence Thomas with a score of 0 percent. In the eight church-state cases heard by Douglas after Warren became chief justice, Douglas voted to expand religious liberty either by enlarging religious free exercise or by outlawing an unconstitutional establishment of religion.[5] By contrast, Thomas has so far heard thirteen cases, and in no case did he vote to expand religious liberty. In all probability he would not even acknowledge the legal standing of a "conscience."

Combining the scores of all justices sitting under each of the last three chief justices shows that the Court under Earl Warren (1953–1969) was the most separationist (liberal) with an average score of 67 percent. Under Chief Justice Warren Burger (1969–1986), the average dropped to 50 percent, where it has stayed under Chief Justice William Rehnquist (1986–) if all fourteen justices serving under him thus far are counted. Five of these, however, have since retired. Without those five, the average of the 9 justices now on the Court is 40 percent, which is strong evidence that the shift from liberal to conservative in the larger political context is mirrored in the judicial branch, at least where church-state issues are concerned.

One more aspect of these voting records is noteworthy. Since Scalia joined the Court in September 1986, he and Rehnquist have heard twenty-two church-state cases and voted alike in all. In eighteen cases they voted "antiseparationist," twelve as part of the majority, six as part of the minority. The only "separationist" votes they cast were the four cases that were unanimous.

Since Thomas joined the Court in October 1991, he has heard thirteen cases and voted every time with Rehnquist and Scalia. It is truly meaningful to say that these three justices constitute a hard-core, regressive bloc on church-state matters.

Why the Decline in Separationism?

How the U.S. Supreme Court has lost enthusiasm for enlarging the separation of church and state, even to the point of making efforts to narrow that separation and lose sight of "conscience," can be understood at three levels: the personal level, the jurisprudential level, and the philosophical level.

The Personal Level

During his 1964 campaign for the presidency, Barry Goldwater in a speech at the University of Chicago said that recent Supreme Court decisions were "jackassian" (Perlstein 2001: 425).[6] Eisenhower, at the end of his presidency, called his appointment of Earl Warren as chief justice his biggest mistake as president. With the election of Richard Nixon in 1968 came a concerted effort to appoint justices who would challenge New Deal/Warren Court measures. Nixon's first two nominees were blocked by the Senate on the grounds that both, as lower court judges, had written opinions that too often were overturned by higher courts. Moreover, the two were tainted with scandal, the first for having heard a case involving a company in which he owned stock, the second for his record of running for office as a white supremacist. The appointment of Warren Burger in 1969 as chief justice brought in a church-state conservative (separationist score: 24 percent), as did the appointments of Lewis Powell (40 percent) and Rehnquist (10 percent). Believing Harry Blackmun to be conservative enough, Nixon was no doubt surprised at how "separationist" Blackmun proved to be (score: 67 percent). Blackmun was also the author of the *Roe v. Wade* decision.

President Ford had a similar experience with naming John Paul Stevens to the Court, for he proved to be a staunch defender of church-state separation (score: 66 percent). President Carter served his four years without any vacancy occurring on the Court.

Like Nixon, Ronald Reagan was clear about his wish to nominate conservatives to the Court. Sandra Day O'Connor (score: 38 percent) and Anthony Kennedy (score: 25 percent) have chiefly lived up to Reagan's expectations, as has Antonin Scalia (score: 24 percent). President George H. W. Bush filled two seats, one with David Souter, who later must have shocked him (score: 65 percent). The other seat went to Clarence Thomas, who may be remembered not only for the grilling he had before the Senate Judiciary Committee but also for seeming to be little more than a rubber stamp for Justice Scalia.

President Clinton named two justices, Ruth Bader Ginsburg and Stephen G. Breyer, whose scores are 83 percent and 58 percent, respectively.

In his 2000 campaign, President George W. Bush indicated, when asked, that he would choose to appoint as Supreme Court justices people like Scalia and Thomas, thus declaring his intention of furthering the move toward regressivism on the Court.

In sum, the Court has declined in its separationist stance because an increasingly conservative executive branch and an increasingly conservative legislative branch have been nominating and approving increasingly conservative persons to serve in the judicial branch. William Brennan (score: 71 percent), appointed by Eisenhower in 1956, and Thurgood Marshall (score: 78 percent), appointed by Johnson in 1967, were the last two nominees to fit the mold of the Earl Warren Court. Marshall's retirement and replacement with Clarence Thomas symbolizes well the profundity of the transition from a Warren Court to a Rehnquist Court. The free exercise of conscience is in jeopardy.

The current Court is very divided, as seen in its frequent 5–4 decisions and not just on church and state. Linda Greenhouse, who covers the Court for the *New York Times*, reports that in the 79 cases handed down during its 2000–2001 term, the Court split 5–4 about one-third of the time (July 15, 2001: 4–5). As a rule, the regressive bloc of three (Rehnquist, Scalia, Thomas) were on the winning or losing side against a progressive bloc of four (Stevens, Souter, Ginsburg, Breyer), the outcomes thus depending upon how two "swing" justices (O'Connor, Kennedy) voted.[7]

Depending upon the jurisprudential outlook of the next few appointees, therefore, the Supreme Court may maintain, even extend, the thrust of Warren Court decision making, or else succeed in further reducing that thrust and undo much that earlier Courts did to protect individual rights, including religious liberty.

The Jurisprudential Level

Stephen Gottlieb (2000: 63), a harsh critic of the Court, says: "The Rehnquist Court has worked a revolution with respect to the underlying jurisprudence of American law. . . . It remains to be seen whether we can, will, or will want to live with it."

But what would result from this 'revolution' were it to be fully effected?

One succinct answer is that the Rehnquist Court would overturn many, if not all, of the New Deal/Warren Court decisions, especially if Gottlieb is correct in his analysis of the Rehnquist Court. He continues (2000: 197): "What unites the core of the conservative group on the Court has been a skepticism about law and government and a hostility toward the underdogs who seek their protection. But they can't say that."

Speaking especially about the regressive bloc of three, he goes on (2000: 35):

> [For them] law is simply and properly a matter of following commands. In turn, the commands are understood directly from the language [of the Constitution] or from historical examples. There is no need to explore the effect of changed circumstances on how the draftsmen [of the Constitution] would have reacted.

Gottlieb's generalization certainly applies in the church-state area.

Some conservatives embrace libertarianism, which leads them to uphold personal autonomy and defend against government efforts to curtail the liberty of individuals. This is true of the so-called neoconservatives, most of whom are former liberals, many having come out of the radical left movements of the 1930s and 1940s. Nonlibertarian conservatives, however, justify their choices in terms either of "democratic" values (i.e., defer to the majority) or "traditional" values (the justification employed by so-called Theocons such as evangelical Christians who would impose their alleged biblical values on others).[8] The regressive bloc on the current Supreme Court, while not particularly sympathetic to religion, are not libertarian either and readily defer to states' rights and elected officials (i.e., majorities) on religion-related issues. As a result of this deference, if a legislature, under pressure from Theocons, voted to reinstate school-sponsored prayer, the bloc would not object, at least on jurisprudential grounds.

In the church-state area, this jurisprudential outlook has led to a remarkable insensitivity to the variety of religious perspectives found in America. Richard Brisbin (1992: 74) says it well:

> Because these justices indicated a preference for popular values and conceptions of religion influenced by Christian religious institutionalism and because they believed that a law constructed by a majority is neutral, they were not sensitive to . . . religious differences. . . . [For example] . . . in *Smith* the Court failed to consider the values of rituals disparate from . . . mainstream denominations. [Use of peyote in the Native American Church] [T]he majority of the Rehnquist Court has been unable to grasp the significance of religious exercises stemming from a cosmology and a cosmogony that offer different perspectives on time, space, logic, order, and ethics. [By permitting a logging road to be built on ground held sacred by Native Americans.] [I]n *O'Lone* the Rehnquist court majority evidenced an inability to understand the importance of a religion's conceptualization of unity, community, and social obligations for its members. . . . [By denying Muslim prisoners in a work gang outside the prison the right to return to prison for Friday noontime prayers.]

These cases, and others like them, close rather than open the gap between church and state. They are refusals to acknowledge the sanctity of conscience. For example, consider the fate of the Warren Court's Sherbert test. As we saw in chapter 5, after deciding a number of free-exercise cases in an ad hoc fashion, the Court in 1963 heard *Sherbert v. Vernon*, during which a strategy was devised for deciding that case and subsequent free exercise cases. We noted that the Sherbert test does not dictate a separationist decision; it is merely a *method* for arriving at a decision. Nonetheless, the Rehnquist bloc wants to do away with the Sherbert test.

They have partly succeeded. In 1990 in *Employment Division v. Smith*, the Court voted 6–3 to uphold the denial of unemployment compensation to two Native American drug counselors who had admitted their use of peyote in the Native American Church ritual, were fired from their jobs, and thus applied for the compensation. Justice Scalia, writing for the majority, cited the reviled *Gobitis* decision as precedent, even though that decision was reversed in 1943, as noted in chapter 5. Scalia said that the Oregon legislation, in outlawing peyote, had not targeted Native Americans and thus the law was "neutral," and all Oregonians must abide by the command. The state was not obligated to give a compelling reason for enforcing the law, *even though it burdened the appellants' free exercise of religion.*

Justice O'Connor hypocritically voted with the majority, even though she balked at dispensing with the compelling interest criterion. She thus in part agreed with (without joining) the dissenting opinion of the three other justices, leaving a majority of five out of nine who were announcing the demise of the Sherbert test.

Court watchers and religious groups were dumbfounded and alarmed at this turn of events. Its effect was to overturn what had become the free-exercise doctrine. Since *Reynolds*, government had been able to restrict religious action, but in doing so, the Court said, government was *required* to justify the restriction; now, following *Smith*, government would have vast power to restrict religious action provided only that the restriction was not aimed specifically at religion. In his zeal to reduce the "legislative" function of the Supreme Court, Scalia had dismantled a long-established understanding of religious liberty in the United States. The balance between legitimate government interests in maintaining social order and individual rights was tipped decidedly in favor of the government and against the right of religious free exercise.

By November 1993, Congress had passed, and President Clinton had signed, the Religious Freedom Restoration Act (RFRA). The heart of the act states that government may not "substantially burden" a person's exercise of religion unless it demonstrates that application of the burden to the person (1) is in furtherance of a compelling governmental interest and (2) is the least restrictive means of furthering that compelling interest.

It is obvious that Congress wanted the Sherbert test restored. It is just as clear that a majority of Supreme Court justices saw RFRA as a congressional usurpation of the judicial branch's power. Ever since *Marbury v. Madison* in 1803, it is the Supreme Court that has determined the constitutionality of legislative acts. Thus, in 1997, the Supreme Court declared RFRA unconstitutional.

The case was *Boerne v. Flores*. The Roman Catholic Church in Boerne, Texas, had outgrown its building and wanted to expand. Its building was in a "historic zone" regulated by special rules that, the city stated, prevented the church from expanding. Archbishop Flores argued that, under RFRA, Boerne could restrict the church's expansion only if it had a compelling interest in doing so. The city responded that there was no requirement to present a compelling interest because RFRA itself was unconstitutional. In *Boerne v. Flores* the Supreme Court agreed with the city. The case did little to clarify free-exercise jurisprudence. At issue, where the Supreme Court was concerned, was RFRA, thus making that case more a referendum on judicial decision making than a free-exercise question. That leaves the future of free-exercise jurisprudence hotly contested and very much up in the air.

The situation is similar with respect to establishment cases. In the 1971 *Lemon v. Kurtzman* decision the Court, under Warren Burger, unanimously struck down two somewhat different plans by states to aid parochial schools financially. In so doing, it articulated what came to be called the "Lemon test," which, like the Sherbert test, consists of three questions: Is the practice being challenged a result of government's *intention* either to aid or inhibit religion? Is aid to or inhibition of religion nonetheless the *effect*? Does the method by which the answer to the second question is known lead to an "entanglement" of government and religion? (For example, is government monitoring required to ensure compliance?) Like the Sherbert test, the Lemon test does not predetermine the decision but is only a strategy for arriving at a decision. Unlike the Sherbert test, however, the Lemon test has led to seemingly contradictory decisions, especially in the area of state aid to private education. The regressive bloc on the current Court would abolish the Lemon test, with the result, no doubt, that states and communities would have greater freedom to do what they wish. For ardent separationists this prospect is frightening, and the status of "conscience" would be in doubt.

There is further cause for alarm. All five of the justices who took it on themselves to make George W. Bush the forty-third president of the United States were on record as "devolutionists"— holding to the jurisprudential principle that higher levels of political power should grant as much freedom as possible to lower levels on the grounds that greater wisdom is found in the grass roots. This may be so on many issues but certainly not when it comes to rights guaranteed by the Constitution, as the issues of slavery and racial segregation gruesomely demonstrated. In essence, this bloc objects to the incorporation of the rights spelled out in the First Amendment into the Fourteenth Amendment. While they acknowledge that the *federal* government is prohibited from restricting free exercise and from passing laws establishing religion, they presumably would have no objection to *state* laws that infringed on religious liberty—at the very least, they would deny the federal government the power to intervene in the states on behalf of citizens whose rights were thus violated. These justices, instead, would leave such unjust laws alone until those whose rights are being violated are able to persuade a majority to change the law through "democratic means." In other words, the justices would gladly submit the rights to "life, liberty, and property" to the popular vote—precisely what the Fifth and Fourteenth Amendments are designed to prevent.

David Shapiro, a Harvard law professor, remarks on the perversity of this jurisprudence in an analysis of Rehnquist's opinions (1976: 293, 298; quoted in Taylor, 2002: 43):

> Too often, unyielding insistence on a particular result appears to have contributed to a widespread discrepancy between theory and practice in matters of constitutional interpretation, to unwarranted relinquishment of federal responsibilities and deference to state laws and institutions, to tacit abandonment of evolving protections of liberty and property, to sacrifice of craftsmanship, and to distortion of precedent.

Hypocrisy characterizes much of the conservative bloc's "jurisprudence." Mention has been made of Scalia's majority opinion in *Smith* in which he cites as precedent the *Gobitis* case that upheld mandatory flag saluting. In doing so, however, he failed to say that, while the *Gobitis* vote was 8–1, this decision was reversed just three years later by a vote of 6–3 in *West Virginia Board of Education v. Barnette*. Scalia's hypocrisy can also be seen in the 2003 *Lawrence v. Texas* case that ruled unconstitutional the Texas law against sodomy. In his dissent, joined by Rehnquist and Thomas, Scalia writes: "The Court has chosen today to revise the standards of *stare decisis* set forth in *Casey* [an abortion case]. It has thereby exposed *Casey's* extraordinary deference to precedent for the result-oriented expedient that it is."

Perhaps Scalia simply forgot what he wrote and did *not* write in *Smith*. His dissent included some telling clichés: "homosexual agenda," "culture war," equating sodomy with "bestiality, adultery, and masturbation." He gratuitously added: "Many Americans do not want persons who openly engage in homosexual conduct as partners in their businesses, as scoutmasters for their children, or as boarders in their homes." Anna Quindlen in her *Newsweek* column (July 14, 2003) responded: "Tweak that sentence to read 'persons who openly engage in Islam' and see how it reads as a high-court opinion in an allegedly free country."

As we said above, the regressive bloc has a hard time with American ideas about liberty and individual rights.

In *his* dissenting opinion, Thomas says that Texas's law against sodomy is "uncommonly silly," but, unable to find in the Constitution any "general right to privacy" or "liberty of the person," he is, he says, not empowered to "to find that law unconstitutional." Of course, Thomas knows of precedents for a right to privacy[9] so, like Scalia, he just invents his reasons and adds to the hypocrisy.

Many more instances could be brought to bear on the regressive bloc's intellectually and ideologically biased jurisprudence, but it is time to move on to the philosophical level, where we shall see how it is that the bloc seems to live in a different world.

The Philosophical Level

Ardent separationists believe they correctly understand what the Framers of the Declaration of Independence and the U.S. Constitution meant by their choice of words, but so do their judicial opponents. No one, of course, would knowingly admit to violating the meaning of these two documents, indicating that, as divided as they are, regressives and progressives on the Supreme Court differ profoundly on the *philosophical* level about what the controlling legal documents of America say.

The liberal position is something like this: In rejecting the legitimacy of King George III's rule, at least most of the leading colonists believed it was possible to create a government capable of ensuring certain "unalienable rights." By unalienable they meant "natural" rights or rights inherent in the nature of human beings, rights that cannot be taken away because they are part of what being human *is*. They are rights that exist *prior* to any design of government and thus are not of human invention; they are even transcendent or sacred. Thus, the Declaration identifies—as self-evident truths—the "natural" rights to life, liberty, and the pursuit of happiness. And the Constitution is the plan for realizing those rights. (As we shall see, regressives on the Court do not agree.)

With this goal in mind as the reason to have a government, the Framers of the U.S. Constitution were faced with an excruciating dilemma—the existence in the colonies of slaves. To interpret the right to life and liberty in the Declaration as outlawing slavery, or to prohibit slavery in the Constitution, would, it was believed, doom the cause of the Revolutionary War: the "nation's" independence from England (West 1997: chapter 1).

Abolitionists went along, convinced of the rightness of their view even if its vindication had to wait. Vindication did come later in the form of a Civil War, fought not just to end slavery but to preserve "one nation" that would strive to live up to the *meaning* of its Constitution, even if evidence was abundant that separating from England and adopting a governmental master plan did not, by themselves, achieve the goals set out in the Declaration.

The *Plessy v. Ferguson* decision of 1896 was an opportunity, following the Civil War, for the U.S. Supreme Court to extend the meaning of the Declaration's commitment to "life" and "liberty," but it chose instead to uphold "separate but equal" facilities for black Americans.

The progressive view therefore sees in the 1954 desegregation of schools decision (*Brown v. Board of Education*) not only something gloriously American but also something faithful to the "original intent" of the Framers.

Against this unfolding of events is another script. It goes like this: Had the Framers intended to outlaw slavery, they would have said and done so. Had the Congress that approved the Thirteenth and Fourteenth Amendments (that did away with slavery) intended to put white and black schoolchildren together, why did that same legislature sustain segregated schools in the District of Columbia?

This regressive perspective, therefore, also claims to adhere to the Founders' "original intent," but it does not see the Constitution as capable of an expanding interpretation of that intent, as the progressives would have it. Thus regressives on the Court acknowledge that the Constitution, as amended, did away with slavery, because this was done legislatively when the states ratified the amendments. Those who see those amendments as a constitutional guarantee of *other* rights are mistaken, regressives believe; they believe that is the task of legislatures. Or, to cite another example, the basis of the abortion decision, *Roe v. Wade*, was the constitutional right to "privacy," but Court regressives reject that reasoning on the grounds that nowhere in the Constitution, including the Fourteenth Amendment, does the word "privacy" appear.

Justice Scalia, writing in dissent to the Texas sodomy case (*Lawrence et al. v. Texas*, 2003) goes even further: "there is no right to 'liberty' under the Due Process Clause." He finds only the right not to be deprived of liberty *without* due process. The Fourteenth Amendment, in Scalia's mind, concerns only *means* by which one may be deprived of liberty; the concept of liberty, evidently, has no substance. Furthermore, majority rule qualifies as a legitimate means of depriving people of their liberty. The onus, in Scalia's mind—and, one must presume, also in the minds of

Rehnquist and Thomas who joined Scalia in the dissent—is on citizens to demonstrate why they have the liberty to act; the government need not give a compelling reason for restricting that liberty. That leaves citizens subject to arbitrary decisions by voting majorities, whose judgment, American history readily shows, is easily swayed by demagogues—loud-mouthed radicals who make use of popular prejudice and fear to promote their agenda. The popular vote is poor protection for freedom, but it qualifies as "due process" for the regressive bloc.

In a way, this difference between progressivism and regressivism is puzzling because adherence to the "natural rights" doctrine has historically been associated more with conservatives than with liberals; traditionalists versus radicals; theists versus secular humanists; absolutists versus relativists. But these dichotomies do not apply in the arena of the philosophy of law. Why? Because the concept of the "natural rights" underlying the Declaration and Constitution is seen by progressive liberals as *inherently malleable in its meaning and application if not in its wording.* The concept is anchored not in "religion" as commonly understood but in individualism and the inviolability of individual conscience. Indeed, in this view, *failure* to allow the Constitution to expand in its meaning and application is a violation of the Constitution itself. Those who imagine this conception of natural rights to be an analog of, say, the Thomistic conception of natural law are mistaken. And those who fail to see the "conscience" roots of the U.S. Constitution—what some regard as a "secular" document, devoid of a sacred element—are also mistaken. Barbara A. McGraw meticulously discusses this issue, and the importance of John Locke as a major influence on the Framers. She is quoted here at some length because she so concisely frames the issue:

> Locke provided the formative foundation and language that shaped the American revolutionary mind and emboldened the American spirit.
>
> Not all agree with this assessment, however. Locke's influence on the American Revolution has been questioned in recent years by those who eschew America's "secular" foundation. In an effort to reclaim the religious roots of America, many are reconsidering the myth of America's founding by

"deists" and maintaining instead that it was evangelical sentiments, not the "rational philosophy" of the likes of John Locke,
that fed the revolutionary goal of the late eighteenth century.

But this assessment is based on the erroneous idea that
Locke's views had little or no religious import. As we have
seen, however, Locke's views were inspired by his "authentic
piety," his political thought is religiously grounded. . . .

Locke's works became the inspiration for impassioned
church sermons that linked freedom to God and advocated
"natural rights," the "social compact," and the right, even the
duty, to resist oppressive arbitrary government. The cause of
individual liberty, infused with Locke's ideas, his language, his
"authentic piety," became a religious cause. . . .

For Locke . . . the traditions and customs of religion gave
way to an individualistic religion—a reliance on individual
conscience imbued with God discovered through reason and
insight. That view led Locke to the conclusion that the only legitimate government is one created by mutual consent of the
people so that individual conscience imbued with God would
remain free, and never legitimately be infringed by government. (2003: 61, 63, 64, 65)

The U.S. Constitution, in other words, is fundamentally a
"sacred," not "secular" document. The basic unit it protects is the
individual conscience, which—to be kept inviolate—requires the
freedom to be exercised as one wills, free from the interference of
the state. Hence the separationist interpretation as it unfolded
during two centuries, culminating in the Warren Court, is fundamentally faithful to the ends ("intent") held by the Framers.
Those Framers, in the words of Mark DeWolfe Howe, aimed at
"converting the limited principle of tolerance into the radical
principle of liberty" (1950: 170–72). The regressive bloc aims to
reverse this process by restoring the limited principle of tolerance. That, we have seen, is the nonpreferentialists' position. It is
thoroughly un-American and not at all "original intent."

Conclusion

It is clear that the regressive bloc currently on the U.S. Supreme
Court does not accept this interpretation of church-state history.

As Gottlieb (2000: xi, 191) puts it:

> In part, the culture war over the Constitution is a war about fidelity to the principles of the Enlightenment that put civilized, humane values ahead of parochial, clannish ones, ahead of values that lead to conflict and the subjugation of one group by another. . . . The conservative bloc has chosen to reject two basic principles of the Anglo-American tradition: the principle that law should be guided by the objective of doing no harm, and the principle of respect for individual moral autonomy where harm to others is not at stake.

Or, as Ronald Dworkin (1996: 125) says of Rehnquist and Scalia:

> They insist that the rights set out in the Constitution, including the right that liberty not be limited except by due process of law, are only a set of discrete rules which neither appeal to nor presuppose any more general principles. They say that the force of these rights is limited to the highly specific expectations of the politicians who created them, and that the rights therefore must be interpreted so as not to condemn any political practices in general force when they were adopted.

If, as seems reasonable, we regard William Rehnquist as the spokesman for the regressive bloc, we learn that crucial to that bloc's perspective are two principles: (1) The authority of the Constitution is grounded in majority rule rather than on any principle of natural law (Rehnquist 1980). (2) All moral judgments are only "personal"; laws are accepted as just not because of any idea of natural justice but simply because they have been included in a constitution or legislatively enacted (Rehnquist 1976).

In holding these two principles, Rehnquist (joined, we must believe, at least by Scalia and Thomas and at times by Kennedy and/or O'Connor) has turned upside down American history and the fundamental values that make up the American creed. Rehnquist's record is quite clear about this perverted view. As an attorney in Phoenix in the 1960s, he opposed a city ordinance prohibiting racial discrimination in public accommodations, for example. As we have already seen, as a law clerk for Justice Robert Jackson when the Court heard the school desegregation case, Rehnquist was asked by Jackson to write an advisory brief. Incredible as it seems, he advised Jackson that he thought the "separate but equal" doctrine was all that the U.S. Constitution required. The U.S. Supreme Court unanimously thought otherwise.[10]

We must assume that Rehnquist does not find slavery *inherently* evil, immoral, or illegal. After the Civil War it became illegal because the Thirteenth Amendment declared it so. Hence, *Plessy v. Ferguson* and its "separate but equal" resolution of the race relations problem is good enough for Rehnquist. But in principle, at least, another constitutional amendment could reinstate slavery, and Rehnquist would not object on legal grounds, certainly not on any notion of natural law. Is it any wonder that Harry Jaffa (1994: 94), a cospeechwriter with Rehnquist for Barry Goldwater in 1964 minces no words:

> The Framers of the Constitution clearly and wisely believed that there must be a lawfulness antecedent to positive law for positive law to be lawful. When Justice Rehnquist says that constitutions do not have any ground in any "idea of natural justice," he is repudiating the Framers. . . . Here we are bound to say, although mortified to say it, that the Chief Justice of the Supreme Court of the United States accuses himself of not understanding the very first premise of the Constitution of the United States.

There is something tragic, and not just alarming, in charging the chief justice of the U.S. Supreme Court with failing to understand "the very first premise" of the U.S. Constitution. The tragedy is compounded by the knowledge that William Rehnquist was, for eighteen months after law school, law clerk to Justice Robert H. Jackson. Jackson is the 1943 author of these words: "The very purpose of the Bill of Rights was to withdraw certain subjects from the vicissitudes of political controversy, to place them beyond the reach of majorities." He was also America's chief prosecutor at the Nuremberg Trials, which most assuredly found Nazi war criminals guilty of violating moral laws that transcend human legislation—in other words, they were found guilty of obeying illegal laws.

We must assume that Chief Justice Rehnquist disbelieves his mentor and finds no warrant for the Nuremberg trials. He joins other regressives in this repudiation of the real intent of not just the Framers and Ratifiers but all who remain faithful to an American creed that expands, rather than shrinks, liberty. He, and others sharing his views, are apostates to the American creed.

Notes

1. Portions of this chapter are drawn, with permission, from Phillip E. Hammond, "What's Happening in American Church/State Separation?" in *Challenging Religion*, ed. J. Beckford and J. Richardson (London: Routledge, 2003) , 129–41.

2. The New Deal is detailed in a large literature, but Steve Fraser and Gary Gerstle's *Rise and Fall of the New Deal Order* (1989) is especially helpful.

3. See also Schulman, *The Seventies: The Great Shift in American Culture, Society, and Politics* (2001). Lucas Powe (2000: xv) writes, "Scholars seem agreed that the Warren Court consisted of a group of powerful, talented men who were more sympathetic to claims of individual liberty, while being simultaneously more egalitarian than their predecessors, more willing to intervene in contentious controversies, more prone to ignore the past, and more convinced that national solutions were superior to local solutions."

4. See appendix 2 for the scores of all the Supreme Court justices from the Earl Warren Court to 2003.

5. Douglas came on the Court in 1939. From then until Earl Warren became chief justice in 1953, Douglas heard sixteen other church-state cases in which he typically voted a separationist line.

6. William Rehnquist, then an attorney in Phoenix, codrafted that speech, though whether the neologism was his or Goldwater's is not mentioned. The other codrafter was Harry Jaffa, a disciple of Leo Strauss, who is a hero to the Neoconservatives. Jaffa, incidentally, wrote the most memorable line in Goldwater's 1964 acceptance speech: "I would remind you that extremism in the defense of liberty is no vice. And let me remind you also that moderation in the pursuit of justice is no virtue" (Perlstein 2001: 391).

7. In December 2000, those swing justices voted with the conservative bloc to declare George W. Bush president in a decision (*Bush v. Gore*) that nearly all Americans who follow Supreme Court actions recognized as

hypocrisy in the extreme. Harvard Law professor Alan Dershowitz (2001: 93) writes that the five justices "were willing not just to *ignore* their own long-held judicial philosophies but to *contradict* them . . . in order to elect the presidential candidate they preferred" (emphasis in the original). We see later why hypocrisy is built into the conservative bloc's philosophy; they have a hard time with American ideas about liberty and individual rights.

8. The term "Theocon" was coined by Jacob Heilbunn (1996: 20–24).

9. As in the *Griswold* case that ruled against Connecticut's ban on the sale of contraceptives and *Roe v. Wade* that found a right to abortion on the grounds of the right to privacy.

10. These anecdotes are contained in Derek Davis (1991: 6–7).

Conclusion

Justice Wiley B. Rutledge, writing for the majority in a 1944 case (*Prince v. Commonwealth of Massachusetts*, in which the Court denied a Jehovah's Witness's free-exercise claim to exemption from child labor laws), remarked:

> [I]t may be doubted that any of the great liberties insured by the First Article [Amendment] can be given higher place than the others. All have preferred position in our basic scheme. . . . All are interwoven there together. Differences there are, in them and in the modes appropriate for their exercise. But they have unity in the charter's prime place because they have unity in their human sources and functionings. Heart and mind are not identical. Intuitive faith and reasoned judgment are not the same. Spirit is not always thought. But in the everyday business of living, secular or otherwise, these variant aspects of personality find inseparable expression in a thousand ways. They cannot be altogether parted in law more than in life.

Justice Rutledge was arguing that the First Amendment freedoms stem from a common source, a source that we have identified as the "freedom of conscience." Furthermore, as we have maintained throughout the book, the freedom of conscience does not derive from our particular system of government; it is, rather, an aspect "of personality." The First Amendment does not "create" the freedom of conscience or the rights derived

151

therefrom; it merely recognizes and respects those rights that we have inherently because a free conscience is in the very nature of what it means to be human.

Clearly, there are circumstances that call for restricting behavior based on individuals' conscientious judgments, such as when conscience-based actions harm others or threaten the public safety. Religious freedom, as we have seen, is not absolute. However, the principles on which the United States was founded, principles that remain—we believe—valid today, demand that freedom not be *arbitrarily* restricted. When the regressive justices, in the name of majority rule, argue that the extent and limits of the free exercise of conscience can be made subject to the legislative process, they introduce the possibility of arbitrary restrictions on what must be considered one of our most sacred freedoms, and we find this abhorrent. It is one thing to prune the diseased branches of liberty; it is another thing entirely to tear at its roots.

When the regressive justices on the Supreme Court today accuse their more progressive colleagues of "creating new rights" whenever a case is not decided to their own liking, they accuse themselves of ignorance of the philosophical basis of the First Amendment. It is shocking to find such ignorance of the principles of liberty among justices of the U.S. Supreme Court; it is alarming to know that President Bush, if reelected in 2004, plans to appoint more justices like them.

Can these challenges be met? It will depend of course on the next one or two appointments to the U.S. Supreme Court. If the conservatives prevail and regressive jurisprudence wins, then as Stephen Gottlieb said above, "It remains to be seen whether we can, will, or will want to live with it."

Appendix 1

To the Honorable General Assembly of the Commonwealth of Virginia a Memorial and Remonstrance

We the subscribers, citizens of the said Commonwealth, having taken into serious consideration, a Bill printed by order of the last Session of General Assembly, entitled "A Bill establishing a provision for Teachers of the Christian Religion," and conceiving that the same if finally armed with the sanctions of a law, will be a dangerous abuse of power, are bound as faithful members of a free State to remonstrate against it, and to declare the reasons by which we are determined. We remonstrate against the said Bill,

1. Because we hold it for a fundamental and undeniable truth, "that Religion or the duty which we owe to our Creator and the manner of discharging it, can be directed only by reason and conviction, not by force or violence." [Virginia Declaration of Rights, art. 16] The Religion then of every man must be left to the conviction and conscience of every man; and it is the right of every man to exercise it as these may dictate. This right is in its nature an unalienable right. It is unalienable, because the opinions of men, depending only on the evidence contemplated by their own minds cannot follow the dictates of other men: It is unalienable also, because what is here a right towards men, is a duty towards the Creator. It is the duty of every man to render to the Creator such homage and such only as he believes to be

acceptable to him. This duty is precedent, both in order of time and in degree of obligation, to the claims of Civil Society. Before any man can be considered as a member of Civil Society, he must be considered as a subject of the Governour of the Universe: And if a member of Civil Society, who enters into any subordinate Association, must always do it with a reservation of his duty to the General Authority; much more must every man who becomes a member of any particular Civil Society, do it with a saving of his allegiance to the Universal Sovereign. We maintain therefore that in matters of Religion, no mans right is abridged by the institution of Civil Society and that Religion is wholly exempt from its cognizance. True it is, that no other rule exists, by which any question which may divide a Society, can be ultimately determined, but the will of the majority; but it is also true that the majority may trespass on the rights of the minority.

2. Because if Religion be exempt from the authority of the Society at large, still less can it be subject to that of the Legislative Body. The latter are but the creatures and vicegerents of the former. Their jurisdiction is both derivative and limited: it is limited with regard to the co-ordinate departments, more necessarily is it limited with regard to the constituents. The preservation of a free Government requires not merely, that the metes and bounds which separate each department of power be invariably maintained; but more especially that neither of them be suffered to overleap the great Barrier which defends the rights of the people. The Rulers who are guilty of such an encroachment, exceed the commission from which they derive their authority, and are Tyrants. The People who submit to it are governed by laws made neither by themselves nor by an authority derived from them, and are slaves.

3. Because it is proper to take alarm at the first experiment on our liberties. We hold this prudent jealousy to be the first duty of Citizens, and one of the noblest characteristics of the late Revolution. The free men of America did not wait till usurped power had strengthened itself by exercise, and entangled the question in precedents. They saw all the consequences in the principle, and they avoided the consequences by denying the principle. We revere this lesson too much soon to forget it. Who does not

see that the same authority which can establish Christianity, in exclusion of all other Religions, may establish with the same ease any particular sect of Christians, in exclusion of all other Sects? that the same authority which can force a citizen to contribute three pence only of his property for the support of any one establishment, may force him to conform to any other establishment in all cases whatsoever?

4. Because the Bill violates that equality which ought to be the basis of every law, and which is more indispensable, in proportion as the validity or expediency of any law is more liable to be impeached. If "all men are by nature equally free and independent," [Virginia Declaration of Rights, art. 1] all men are to be considered as entering into Society on equal conditions; as relinquishing no more, and therefore retaining no less, one than another, of their natural rights. Above all are they to be considered as retaining an "equal title to the free exercise of Religion according to the dictates of Conscience." [Virginia Declaration of Rights, art. 16] Whilst we assert for ourselves a freedom to embrace, to profess and to observe the Religion which we believe to be of divine origin, we cannot deny an equal freedom to those whose minds have not yet yielded to the evidence which has convinced us. If this freedom be abused, it is an offence against God, not against man: To God, therefore, not to man, must an account of it be rendered. As the Bill violates equality by subjecting some to peculiar burdens, so it violates the same principle, by granting to others peculiar exemptions. Are the Quakers and Menonists the only sects who think a compulsive support of their Religions unnecessary and unwarrantable? Can their piety alone be entrusted with the care of public worship? Ought their Religions to be endowed above all others with extraordinary privileges by which proselytes may be enticed from all others? We think too favorably of the justice and good sense of these denominations to believe that they either covet pre-eminences over their fellow citizens or that they will be seduced by them from the common opposition to the measure.

5. Because the Bill implies either that the Civil Magistrate is a competent Judge of Religious Truth; or that he may employ Religion as an engine of Civil policy. The first is an arrogant pretension

falsified by the contradictory opinions of Rulers in all ages, and throughout the world: the second an unhallowed perversion of the means of salvation.

6. Because the establishment proposed by the Bill is not requisite for the support of the Christian Religion. To say that it is, is a contradiction to the Christian Religion itself, for every page of it disavows a dependence on the powers of this world: it is a contradiction to fact; for it is known that this Religion both existed and flourished, not only without the support of human laws, but in spite of every opposition from them, and not only during the period of miraculous aid, but long after it had been left to its own evidence and the ordinary care of Providence. Nay, it is a contradiction in terms; for a Religion not invented by human policy, must have pre-existed and been supported, before it was established by human policy. It is moreover to weaken in those who profess this Religion a pious confidence in its innate excellence and the patronage of its Author; and to foster in those who still reject it, a suspicion that its friends are too conscious of its fallacies to trust it to its own merits.

7. Because experience witnesseth that ecclesiastical establishments, instead of maintaining the purity and efficacy of Religion, have had a contrary operation. During almost fifteen centuries has the legal establishment of Christianity been on trial. What have been its fruits? More or less in all places, pride and indolence in the Clergy, ignorance and servility in the laity, in both, superstition, bigotry and persecution. Enquire of the Teachers of Christianity for the ages in which it appeared in its greatest lustre; those of every sect, point to the ages prior to its incorporation with Civil policy. Propose a restoration of this primitive State in which its Teachers depended on the voluntary rewards of their flocks, many of them predict its downfall. On which Side ought their testimony to have greatest weight, when for or when against their interest?

8. Because the establishment in question is not necessary for the support of Civil Government. If it be urged as necessary for the support of Civil Government only as it is a means of supporting Religion, and it be not necessary for the latter purpose, it cannot be necessary for the former. If Religion be not within the cognizance of Civil Government how can its legal establishment

be necessary to Civil Government? What influence in fact have ecclesiastical establishments had on Civil Society? In some instances they have been seen to erect a spiritual tyranny on the ruins of the Civil authority; in many instances they have been seen upholding the thrones of political tyranny: in no instance have they been seen the guardians of the liberties of the people. Rulers who wished to subvert the public liberty, may have found an established Clergy convenient auxiliaries. A just Government instituted to secure & perpetuate it needs them not. Such a Government will be best supported by protecting every Citizen in the enjoyment of his Religion with the same equal hand which protects his person and his property; by neither invading the equal rights of any Sect, nor suffering any Sect to invade those of another.

9. Because the proposed establishment is a departure from that generous policy, which, offering an Asylum to the persecuted and oppressed of every Nation and Religion, promised a lustre to our country, and an accession to the number of its citizens. What a melancholy mark is the Bill of sudden degeneracy? Instead of holding forth an Asylum to the persecuted, it is itself a signal of persecution. It degrades from the equal rank of Citizens all those whose opinions in Religion do not bend to those of the Legislative authority. Distant as it may be in its present form from the Inquisition, it differs from it only in degree. The one is the first step, the other the last in the career of intolerance. The magnanimous sufferer under this cruel scourge in foreign Regions, must view the Bill as a Beacon on our Coast, warning him to seek some other haven, where liberty and philanthropy in their due extent, may offer a more certain repose from his Troubles.

10. Because it will have a like tendency to banish our Citizens. The allurements presented by other situations are every day thinning their number. To super add a fresh motive to emigration by revoking the liberty which they now enjoy, would be the same species of folly which has dishonoured and depopulated flourishing kingdoms.

11. Because it will destroy that moderation and harmony which the forbearance of our laws to intermeddle with Religion has produced among its several sects. Torrents of blood have been spilt in the old world, by vain attempts of the secular arm, to

extinguish Religious discord, by proscribing all difference in Religious opinion. Time has at length revealed the true remedy. Every relaxation of narrow and rigorous policy, wherever it has been tried, has been found to assuage the disease. The American Theatre has exhibited proofs that equal and compleat liberty, if it does not wholly eradicate it, sufficiently destroys its malignant influence on the health and prosperity of the State. If with the salutary effects of this system under our own eyes, we begin to contract the bounds of Religious freedom, we know no name that will too severely reproach our folly. At least let warning be taken at the first fruits of the threatened innovation. The very appearance of the Bill has transformed "that Christian forbearance, love and charity," [Virginia Declaration of Rights, art. 16] which of late mutually prevailed, into animosities and jealousies, which may not soon be appeased. What mischiefs may not be dreaded, should this enemy to the public quiet be armed with the force of a law?

12. Because the policy of the Bill is adverse to the diffusion of the light of Christianity. The first wish of those who enjoy this precious gift ought to be that it may be imparted to the whole race of mankind. Compare the number of those who have as yet received it with the number still remaining under the dominion of false Religions; and how small is the former! Does the policy of the Bill tend to lessen the disproportion? No; it at once discourages those who are strangers to the light of revelation from coming into the Region of it; and countenances by example the nations who continue in darkness, in shutting out those who might convey it to them. Instead of Leveling as far as possible, every obstacle to the victorious progress of Truth, the Bill with an ignoble and unchristian timidity would circumscribe it with a wall of defence against the encroachments of error.

13. Because attempts to enforce by legal sanctions, acts obnoxious to so great a proportion of Citizens, tend to enervate the laws in general, and to slacken the bands of Society. If it be difficult to execute any law which is not generally deemed necessary or salutary, what must be the case, where it is deemed invalid and dangerous? And what may be the effect of so striking an example of impotency in the Government, on its general authority?

14. Because a measure of such singular magnitude and delicacy ought not to be imposed, without the clearest evidence that it is called for by a majority of citizens, and no satisfactory method is yet proposed by which the voice of the majority in this case may be determined, or its influence secured. "The people of the respective counties are indeed requested to signify their opinion respecting the adoption of the Bill to the next Session of Assembly." But the representation must be made equal, before the voice either of the Representatives or of the Counties will be that of the people. Our hope is that neither of the former will, after due consideration, espouse the dangerous principle of the Bill. Should the event disappoint us, it will still leave us in full confidence, that a fair appeal to the latter will reverse the sentence against our liberties.

15. Because finally, "the equal right of every citizen to the free exercise of his Religion according to the dictates of conscience" is held by the same tenure with all our other rights. If we recur to its origin, it is equally the gift of nature; if we weigh its importance, it cannot be less dear to us; if we consult the "Declaration of those rights which pertain to the good people of Virginia, as the basis and foundation of Government," it is enumerated with equal solemnity, or rather studied emphasis. Either then, we must say, that the Will of the Legislature is the only measure of their authority; and that in the plenitude of this authority, they may sweep away all our fundamental rights; or, that they are bound to leave this particular right untouched and sacred: Either we must say, that they may controul the freedom of the press, may abolish the Trial by Jury, may swallow up the Executive and Judiciary Powers of the State; nay that they may despoil us of our very right of suffrage, and erect themselves into an independent and hereditary Assembly or, we must say, that they have no authority to enact into law the Bill under consideration. We the Subscribers say, that the General Assembly of this Commonwealth have no such authority: And that no effort may be omitted on our part against so dangerous an usurpation, we oppose to it, this remonstrance; earnestly praying, as we are in duty bound, that the Supreme Lawgiver of the Universe, by illuminating those to whom it is addressed, may on the one hand, turn their Councils

from every act which would affront his holy prerogative, or violate the trust committed to them: and on the other, guide them into every measure which may be worthy of his blessing, may redound to their own praise, and may establish more firmly the liberties, the prosperity and the happiness of the Commonwealth.

Act for Establishing Religious Freedom

Well aware that Almighty God hath created the mind free; that all attempts to influence it by temporal punishments or burdens, or by civil incapacitations, tend only to beget habits of hypocrisy and meanness, and are a departure from the plan of the Holy Author of our religion, who being Lord both of body and mind, yet chose not to propagate it by coercions on either, as was in his Almighty power to do; that the impious presumption of legislators and rulers, civil as well as ecclesiastical, who, being themselves but fallible and uninspired men, have assumed dominion over the faith of others, setting up their own opinions and modes of thinking as the only true and infallible, and as such endeavoring to impose them on others, hath established and maintained false religions over the greatest part of the world, and through all time; that to compel a man to furnish contributions of money for the propagation of opinions which he disbelieves, is sinful and tyrannical; that even the forcing him to support this or that teacher of his own religious persuasion, is depriving him of the comfortable liberty of giving his contributions to the particular pastor whose morals he would make his pattern, and whose powers he feels most persuasive to righteousness, and is withdrawing from the ministry those temporal rewards, which proceeding from an approbation of their personal conduct, are an additional incitement to earnest and unremitting labors for the instruction of mankind; that our civil rights have no dependence on our religious opinions, more than our opinions in physics or geometry; that, therefore, the proscribing any citizen as unworthy the public confidence by laying upon him an incapacity of being called to the offices of trust and emolument, unless he profess or renounce this or that religious opinion, is depriving him injuriously of those privileges and advantages to which in common with his fellow citizens he has a natural right; that it tends also to corrupt the principles of that very religion it is meant to encourage, by bribing, with a monopoly of worldly honors and emoluments, those who will externally profess and conform to it; that though indeed these are criminal who do not withstand such temptation, yet neither are those innocent who lay the bait in their way; that to suffer the civil magistrate to intrude his powers into the field of opinion and to restrain the profession or propagation of principles, on the supposition of their ill tendency, is a dangerous fallacy, which at once destroys all religious liberty, because he being of course judge of that tendency, will make his opinions the rule of judgment, and approve or condemn the sentiments of others only as they shall square with or differ from his own; that it is time enough for the rightful purposes of civil government, for its officers to interfere when principles break out into overt acts against peace and good order; and finally, that truth is great and will prevail if left to herself, that she is the proper and sufficient antagonist to error, and has nothing to fear from the conflict, unless by human interposition disarmed of her natural weapons, free argument and debate, errors ceasing to be dangerous when it is permitted freely to contradict them.

Be it therefore enacted by the General Assembly, That no man shall be compelled to frequent or support any religious worship, place, or ministry whatsoever, nor shall be enforced, restrained, molested, or burdened in his body or goods, nor shall otherwise suffer on account of his religious opinions or belief; but that all men shall be free to profess, and by argument to maintain, their opinions in matters of religion, and that the same shall in nowise diminish, enlarge, or affect their civil capacities.

And though we well know this Assembly, elected by the people for the ordinary purposes of legislation only, have no powers equal to our own and that therefore to declare this act irrevocable would be of no effect in law, yet we are free to declare, and do declare, that the rights hereby asserted are of the natural rights of mankind, and that if any act shall be hereafter passed to repeal the present or to narrow its operation, such act will be an infringement of natural right.

Appendix 2

Separationist Votes by U.S. Supreme Court Justices since 1960

Justices	% Separationist Vote (N)	Average
The Warren Court (1953 [1960]–1969)		67%
Earl Warren	63(8)	
Byron White	50(8)	
Hugo Black	75(8)	
Potter Stewart	50(8)	
John M. Harlan	63(8)	
William Brennan	63(8)	
Tom C. Clark	71(7)	
William O. Douglas	100(8)	
The Burger Court (1969–1986)		50%
Warren Burger	24(33)	
Byron White	33(33)	
Hugo Black	67(6)	
Potter Stewart	36(22)	
John M. Harlan	40(5)	
William Brennan	73(33)	
William O. Douglas	100(8)	
Thurgood Marshall	76(33)	
Harry Blackmun	64(33)	
Lewis Powell	40(25)	
Sandra Day O'Connor	40(10)	
William Rehnquist	5(19)	
John Paul Stevens	61(25)	

(continued)

Justices	% Separationist Vote (N)	Average
The Rehnquist Court (1986–)		50%
William Rehnquist	10(29)	
Byron White	39(18)	
William Brennan	77(13)	
Thurgood Marshall	79(14)	
Harry Blackmun	70(20)	
Lewis Powell	40(5)	
Sandra Day O'Connor	38(29)	
John Paul Stevens	66(29)	
Anthony Kennedy	25(24)	
Antonin Scalia	24(29)	
David Souter	65(17)	
Clarence Thomas	0 (21)	
Ruth Bader Ginsburg	83(12)	
David Breyer	58(12)	

Bibliography

Abraham, Henry J., and Barbara A. Perry. 1998. *Freedom and the Court: Civil Rights and Liberties in the United States*, 7th ed. New York: Oxford University Press.

Adams, Arlin M., and Charles J. Emmerich. 1990. *A Nation Dedicated to Religious Liberty: The Constitutional Heritage of the Religion Clauses*. Philadelphia: University of Pennsylvania Press.

Adams, John Stokes, ed. 1937. *An Autobiographical Sketch by John Marshall Written at the Request of Joseph Story and Now Printed for the First Time from the Original Manuscript Preserved at the William L. Clements Library, Together with a Letter from Chief Justice John Marshall to Justice Story Relating Thereto*. Ann Arbor: University of Michigan Press.

Alley, Robert S., ed. 1985. *James Madison on Religious Liberty*. Buffalo, N.Y.: Prometheus Books.

Banner, Stuart. 1998. "When Christianity Was Part of the Common Law." *Law and History Review* 16: 27–62.

Beckford, James A., and James T. Richardson, eds. 2003. *Challenging Religion*. London: Routledge

Borden, Morton. 1984. *Jews, Turks, and Infidels*. Chapel Hill: University of North Carolina Press.

Bowden, Henry Warner. 1981. *American Indians and Christian Missions: Studies in Cultural Conflict*. Chicago: University of Chicago Press.

Brisbin, Richard A. 1992. "The Rehnquist Court and the Free Exercise of Religion." *Journal of Church and State* 34: 74.

Bruce, Steve. 2003. *Politics and Religion*. Malden, Mass.: Blackwell Publishing.

Buckley, William F. 1956. Editorial. *National Review*, 2 (November 3): 6–7

Butler, Jon. 1990. *Awash in a Sea of Faith: Christianizing the American People*. Cambridge, Mass.: Harvard University Press.

Carmela, Angela C. 1993. "The Religion Clauses and Acculturated Religious Conduct: Boundaries for the Regulation of Religion." In *The Role of Government in Monitoring and Regulating Religion in Public Life*, edited by J. R. Wood and D. Davis, 21–49. Waco, Tex.: J. M. Dawson Institute of Church-State Studies.

Carter, Stephen. 1993. *The Culture of Disbelief*. New York: Basic Books.

Commager, Henry Steele. 1953. "Joseph Story." In *The Gaspar G. Bacon Lectures on the Constitution of the United States, 1940–1950*, 33–94. Boston: Boston University Press.

Conkle, Daniel O. 2003. *Constitutional Law: The Religion Clauses*. New York: Foundation Press.

Davis, Derek. 1991. *Original Intent: Chief Justice Rehnquist and the Court of American Church/State Relations*. Buffalo, N.Y.: Prometheus Books.

———. 1993. "The Courts and the Constitutional Meaning of 'Religion': A History and Critique." In *The Role of Government in Monitoring and Regulating Religion in Public Life*, edited by J. R. Wood and D. Davis, 89–119. Waco, Tex.: J. M. Dawson Institute of Church-State Studies.

Dershowitz, Alan. 2001. *Supreme Injustice*. New York: Oxford University Press.

Dowd, Morgan D. 1965. "Justice Joseph Story: A Study of the Legal Philosophy of a Jeffersonian Judge." *Vanderbilt Law Review* 18: 643–62.

Dreisbach, Daniel L. 1996. "In Search of a Christian Commonwealth: An Examination of Selected Nineteenth-Century Commentaries on References to God and the Christian Religion in the United States Constitution." *Baylor Law Review* 48: 927–1001.

Dunne, Gerald T. 1963. "The American Blackstone." *Washington University Law Quarterly* 41: 321–37.

———. 1970. *Justice Joseph Story and the Rise of the Supreme Court*. New York: Simon and Schuster.

Dworkin, Ronald. 1993. *Life's Dominion*. New York: Alfred A. Knopf.

———. 1996. *Freedom's Law*. Cambridge, Mass.: Harvard University Press.

Eskridge, William N. Jr. 1996. *The Case for Same-Sex Marriage*. New York: Free Press.

Flowers, Ronald B. 1994. *That Godless Court?* Louisville, Ky.: Westminster John Knox Press.

Frankel, Marvin E. 1992. "Religion and Public Life: Reasons for Minimal Access." *George Washington Law Review* 60: 633–44.

———. 1994. *Faith and Freedom*. New York: Hill and Wang.

Fraser, Steve, and Gary Gerstle, eds. 1989. *The Rise and Fall of the New Deal Order, 1930–1980*. Princeton, N.J.: Princeton University Press.

Galanter, Marc. 1966. "Religious Freedom in the United States: A Turning Point?" *Wisconsin Law Review* 1966: 217–96.

Gottlieb, Stephen. 2000. *Morality Imposed: The Rehnquist Court and Liberty in America*. New York: New York University Press.

Greenawalt, Kent. 1993. "The Role of Religion in a Liberal Democracy." *Journal of Church and State* 35: 503–19.

Greenhouse, Linda. 2001. "Behind the Court's Civil Rights Ruling." *New York Times*, Week in Review (July 15): 4–5.

Hamilton, Alexander, James Madison, and John Jay. 1961. *The Federalist*. Edited by B. F. Wright. New York: Metro Books.

Hammond, Phillip E. 1998. *With Liberty for All: Freedom of Religion in the United States*. Louisville, Ky.: Westminster John Knox Press.

Handy, Robert T. 1984. *A Christian America: Protestant Hopes and Historical Realities*, 2d ed. New York: Oxford University Press.

———. 1991. *Undermined Establishment: Church-State Relations in America 1880–1920*. Princeton, N.J.: Princeton University Press.

Hatch, Nathan O. 1989. *The Democratization of American Christianity*. New Haven, Conn.: Yale University Press.

Heilbunn, Jacob. 1996. "Neocon v. Theocon." *The New Republic* (December 20): 20–24.

Himmelstein, Jerome L. 1990. *To the Right: The Transformation of American Conservatism*. Berkeley: University of California Press.

Howard, A. E. Dick. 1985. "James Madison and the Founding of the Republic." In *James Madison on Religious Liberty*, edited by R. S. Alley, 21–34. Buffalo, N.Y.: Prometheus Books.

Howe, Mark DeWolf. 1950. "Review of Anson Phelps Stokes, *Church and State in the United States*." *Harvard Law Review* 64: 170–72.

Hutson, James H. 1991. "What are the Rights of the People?" *Wilson Quarterly* (Winter): 57–70.

Ingber, Stanley. 1989. "Religion or Ideology: A Needed Clarification of the Religion Clauses." *Stanford Law Review* 41: 233–333.

Isler, Claudia. 2001. *The Right to Free Speech*. New York: Rosen Publishing Group, Inc.

Jaffa, Harry V. 1994. *Original Intent and the Framers of the Constitution*. Washington, D.C.: Regnery Gateway.

Konefsky, Alfred S. 1988. "Law and Culture in Antebellum Boston [Book Review]." *Stanford Law Review* 40: 1119–47.

Konvitz, Milton R. 1968. *Religious Liberty and Conscience*. New York: Viking Press.

Lerner, Ralph. 1989. "Believers and the Founders' Constitution." *This World* 26: 88–89.

Levinson, Sanford. 1988. *Constitutional Faith*. Princeton, N.J.: Princeton University Press.

Lippy, Charles H. 1978. "The 1780 Massachusetts Constitution: Religious Establishment or Civil Religion?" *Journal of Church and State* 20: 533–49.

Machacek, David W., and Melissa M. Wilcox, eds. 2003. *Sexuality and the World's Religions*. Santa Barbara, Calif.: ABC-CLIO.

Marini, Stephen A. 1994. "Religion, Politics, and Ratification." In *Religion in a Revolutionary Age*, edited by R. Hoffman and P. J. Albert, 184–217. Charlottesville: University Press of Virginia.

Mazur, Eric Michael. 1999. *The Americanization of Religious Minorities: Confronting the Constitutional Order*. Baltimore: Johns Hopkins University Press.

McAninch, William Shepard. 1987. "A Catalyst for the Evolution of Constitutional Law: Jehovah's Witnesses in the Supreme Court." *University of Cincinnati Law Review* 55: 997–1077.

McClellan, James. 1971. *Joseph Story and the American Constitution: A Study in Political and Legal Thought*. Norman: University of Oklahoma Press.

McCloskey, Robert G. 1960. *The American Supreme Court*. Chicago: University of Chicago Press.

McGraw, Barbara A. 2003. *Rediscovering America's Sacred Ground: Public Religion and Pursuit of the Good in a Pluralistic America*. Albany: State University of New York Press.

Miller, Robert T, and Ronald B. Flowers, eds. 1996. *Toward Benevolent Neutrality*, Vol. 2 Waco, Tex.: Baylor University Press.

Miller, William Lee. 1988. *The First Liberty: Religion and the American Republic*. New York: Paragon House Publishers.

Moore, R. Laurence. 1986. *Religious Outsiders and the Making of Americans*. New York: Oxford University Press.

Moskos, Charles C., and John Whiteclay Chambers II, eds. 1993. *The New Conscientious Objection: From Sacred to Secular Resistance*. New York: Oxford University Press.

Neuhaus, Richard John. 1984. *The Naked Public Square*. Grand Rapids, Mich.: William B. Eerdmans.

Newmyer, R. Kent. 1985. *Supreme Court Justice Joseph Story: Statesman of the Old Republic*. Chapel Hill: University of North Carolina Press.

Perlstein, Rick. 2001. *Before the Storm: Barry Goldwater and the Unmaking of the American Consensus*. New York: Hill and Wang.

Peterson, R. Dean. 1993. *A Concise History of Christianity*. Belmont, Calif.: Wadsworth Publishing Company.

Pound, Roscoe. 1914. "The Place of Judge Story in the Making of American Law." *American Law Review* 48: 676–97.

Powe, Lucas. 2000. *The Warren Court and American Politics*. Cambridge, Mass.: Harvard University Press.

Powell, H. Jefferson. 1985. "Joseph Story's *Commentaries on the Constitution*: A Belated Review." *Yale Law Journal* 94: 1285–1314.

Quindlen, Anna. 2003. "Justice Rip Van Winkle." *Newsweek* (July 14): 68.

Rehnquist, William. 1976. "The Notion of a Living Constitution." *Texas Law Review* 54: 693–706.

———. 1980. "Government by Cliché." *Missouri Law Review* 45: 379–93.

Richards, David A. J. 1986. *Toleration and the Constitution*. New York: Oxford University Press.

———. 1999. *Identity and the Case for Gay Rights: Race, Gender, Religion as Analogies*. Chicago: University of Chicago Press.

Rogge, O. John. 1960. *The First and the Fifth with Some Excursions into Others*. New York: Thomas Nelson and Sons.

Rutland, Robert A. 1955. *The Birth of a Bill of Rights, 1776–1791*. Chapel Hill: University of North Carolina Press.

Sarna, Jonathan D. 1990. "Is Judaism Compatible with American Civil Religion? The Problem of Christmas and the 'National Faith.'" In *Religion and the Life of the Nation*, edited by R. A. Sherrill, 152–73. Urbana: University of Illinois Press.

Schulman, Bruce J. 2001. *The Seventies: The Great Shift in American Culture, Society, and Politics*. New York: Free Press.

Schwartz, Bernard, ed. 1971. *The Bill of Rights: A Documentary History*, 2 volumes. New York: Chelsea House.

———. 1995. "Supreme Court Superstars: The Ten Greatest Justices." *Tulsa Law Journal* 31 (Fall): 93–159.

Shapiro, David. 1976. "Mr. Justice Rehnquist: A Preliminary View." *Harvard Law Review* 90: 293–357.

Sherwood, Carlton. 1991. *Inquisition*. Washington, D.C.: Regnery Gateway.

Stevens, Leonard A. 1973. *Salute! The Case of the Bible vs. the Flag*. New York: Putnam.

Stone, Harlan Fiske. 1919. "The Conscientious Objector." *Columbia University Quarterly* 21: 253–69.

Story, Joseph. 1828. *A Discourse Pronounced at the Request of the Essex County Historical Society on the 18th of September, 1828, in Commemoration of the First Settlement of Salem, in the State of Massachusetts*. Boston: Hilliard, Gray, Little, and Wilkins.

———— . [1833] 1970. *Commentaries on the Constitution of the United States*. Reprint. New York: Da Capo Press.

Story, William W., ed. 1851. *Life and Letters of Joseph Story, Associate Justice of the Supreme Court of the United States and Dane Professor of Law at Harvard University*. Boston: Little Brown.

Taylor, William L. 2002. "Racial Equality: The World according to Rehnquist." In *The Rehnquist Court: Judicial Activism on the Right*, edited by H. Schwartz, 39–54. New York: Hill and Wang.

Upshur, Abel P. [1840] 1971. *A Brief Enquiry into the True Nature and Character of Our Federal Government*. Reprint. New York: Da Capo Press.

Waite, Edward F. 1944. "The Debt of Constitutional Law to Jehovah's Witnesses." *Minnesota Law Review* 28: 209–46.

Washington, James M. 1992. "The Crisis in the Sanctity of Conscience in American Jurisprudence." *DePaul Law Review* 42: 11–60.

Way, H. Frank. 1987. "Death of the Christian Nation: The Judiciary and Church-State Relations." *Journal of Church and State* 29: 509–29.

Wenz, Peter. 1992. *Abortion Rights as Religious Freedom*. Philadelphia: Temple University Press.

West, Thomas G. 1997. *Vindicating the Founders*. Lanham, Md.: Rowman & Littlefield.

Wilson, John F. 1990. "Religion, Government, and Power in the New American Nation." *Religion and American Politics: From the Colonial Period to the 1980s*, edited by M. A. Noll, 77–91. New York: Oxford University Press.

Wilson, John F., and Donald L. Drakeman, eds. 2003. *Church and State in American History: Key Documents, Decisions, and Commentary from the Past Three Centuries*, 3d ed. Boulder, Colo.: Westview Press.

Wilson, John K. 1990. "Religion Under the State Constitutions, 1776–1800." *Journal of Church and State* 32: 753–73.

Witte, John Jr. 1999. "'A Most Mild and Equitable Establishment of Religion': John Adams and the Massachusetts Experiment." *Journal of Church and State* 41: 213–52.

Wuthnow, Robert. 1988. *The Restructuring of American Religion: Society and Faith since World War II*. Princeton, N.J.: Princeton University Press.

Index

About the Authors

Phillip E. Hammond is D. Mackenzie Brown Professor Emeritus of Religious Studies at the University of California at Santa Barbara.

David W. Machacek is Resident Fellow at the Greenberg Center for the Study of Religion in Public Life and Visiting Assistant Professor of Public Policy at Trinity College in Hartford, Connecticut.

Eric Michael Mazur is Associate Professor of Religion at Bucknell University in Lewisburg, Pennsylvania.